Young Adult

GERTRUDE KÄSEBIER

Gertrude Käsebier was a pictorialist and founding member of the Photo-Secession movement. Known for her unique photographs of mothers and their daughters, Käsebier was one of the first prominent female photographers. In 1898, she invited other women to take up the study of fine art photography:

I feel diffident in speaking to you about photography, because I have not followed the beaten paths, and because I have had to wade through seas of criticism on account of my heretical views. . . .

The key to artistic photography is to work out your own thoughts, by yourselves. Imitation leads to certain disaster. New ideas are always antagonized. Do not mind that. If a thing is good it will survive. I earnestly advise women of artistic tastes to train for the unworked field of modern photography. It seems to be especially adapted to them, and the few who have entered it are meeting with gratifying and profitable success. If one already draws and paints, so much the better. If one has wrestled with the subtle lines of the human form; if one has experienced the feeling of trying to produce color from simple pigments, their enjoyment of the exquisite pictures thrown upon the ground glass will be enhanced, and their artistic growth and color sense will not suffer.

Quoted in Brooks Johnson, ed., *Photography Speaks: 150 Photographers on Their Art.* New York: Aperture Foundation, 2004, p. 94.

Renoir, Paul Cézanne, and others. Impressionist paintings often depicted ordinary subject matter at unusual angles in a soft or blurred focus, with an exaggerated contrast between light and dark. British photographer Peter Henry Emerson was aware that such qualities lent themselves perfectly to photography, and he expressed this concept in a very influential book, *Naturalistic Photography for Students of Art.*

Emerson stated that people should be photographed as ordinary subject matter, as they really appeared, not dressed up in fancy clothes or striking contrived poses. He also thought that the camera should mimic the human eye, keeping the main subject in sharp focus and the surrounding area much less distinct. However, when it came to nature, Emerson used a different logic. Instead of documenting the natural world in a straight, representative manner, he urged art photographers to use the soft or blurred vision of the impressionist painters.

Emerson's book was quite controversial at the time—one critic compared the author's beliefs to "dropping a bomb at a tea-party."[13] However, *Naturalistic Photography for Students of Art* spawned a popular international photography movement called pictorialism, which required photographers to use a variety of techniques. To produce soft-focus pictures, which depicted objects blurred around the edges, photographers used special filters, such as gauze, or coated their lenses with petroleum jelly. In the darkroom, photographers continued the pictorial process with labor-intensive methods beyond the skills of the amateur. Some made their own hand-coated photographic paper using sheets of expensive, handmade cotton art paper as a base. Or, in order to imitate the defining brush strokes of the impressionists, photographers used rough-surfaced papers or even scratched their prints with tiny needles. Whatever the technique, as influential photographer, author, and curator at Princeton University Peter C. Bunnell writes, two principal concepts of pictorialism were foremost: "Firstly, that making meaningful, expressive photographs required discipline, considerable [concentration], and knowledge of the traditional arts. Secondly, that in matters of craft and artistry, producing a fine photographic print was an act analogous to the creative endeavor in any medium."[14]

The Photo-Secession Movement

By the early twentieth century, photographic pictorialism was recognized throughout the world as a fine art movement. Pictorialist exhibitions attracted large crowds in Milan, Munich,

throughout society. By the early 1840s, throngs of people were gathering daily in front of the first camera shops in Paris. A few brave entrepreneurs came forward with the large sum of 400 francs, equal to six months' salary for a skilled worker to purchase a daguerreotype camera. These early photographers needed the technical skills to complete the complicated chemical process as well as a strong back. The first camera, with its wooden body, lens, and several lightproof boxes where the copper plates could be treated with chemicals, weighed over 100 pounds (45kg).

The First Portrait Studio

Although France provided the world with the first cameras, the daguerreotype process was quickly perfected by two Americans from New York City, Alexander Wolcott and John Johnson. These business partners, who manufactured scientific and dental instruments, bought a camera, read Daguerre's official manual, and began making improvements to the process almost immediately. Wolcott's knowledge of astronomy prompted him to replace Daguerre's lens with a high-quality, polished telescope mirror that intensified the amount of light hitting the photographic plate. This was a major development that reduced daguerreotype exposure times from ten minutes to about thirty seconds. Thus was born the first photographic process that could be used to take portraits. Although the resulting pictures were very small, 2 by 2.5 inches (5 by 6 cm), the *New York Sun* described them as "perfect as nature itself."[3]

On March 15, 1840, Wolcott and Johnson used their superior version of the camera to open in Wolcott's home the world's first portrait studio. Taking a successful daguerreotype, however, required skill on the part of the photographers and patience from the sitter whose portrait was being taken. Even with the improved lens, the daguerreotype still required very bright light, which was beamed from windows onto the sitter's face with large mirrors hung from the ceiling by chains. Despite the illumination method, the sitters could not squint or blink, because if they moved, or even smiled, the photo would be blurred or

Posing for a daguerreotype portrait was no easy task. The sitters would have to remain perfectly still—while maintaining their poses—for upwards of thirty seconds while the photo was being taken.

show indistinct features. To deflect the light for the thirty-second exposure, Wolcott and Johnson placed a blue-tinted glass in front of the sitter, and they used crude cast-iron head clamps or posing stands to keep the sitter immobilized. This system, widely imitated in later years, is the reason that early photographs show goggle-eyed subjects who look extremely stiff and uncomfortable.

When the punishment was over, the sitter was rewarded with a miniature portrait. It took four minutes to develop and cost $5, roughly equivalent to $115 in today's currency. The finished daguerreotype was treated like a precious treasure, mounted behind a protective layer of glass and enclosed in a velvet-lined leather case with a lid that opened and closed like a book.

obscura. Mo Ti wrote that light, passing through a pinhole in a curtain into a dark room, projected an inverted color image of the scene outside onto the opposite wall. Mo Ti called his darkened room a "collecting place" or the "locked treasure room." By the sixteenth century, it was not necessary to have an entire room for a camera obscura. The development of optical lenses and mirrors made it possible to project images onto a much smaller surface inside a portable wooden box. This new version of the camera obscura was the forerunner of the modern camera. Its ability to reflect imagery can be explained by a basic law of physics. Light travels in a straight line, but when the rays pass through a small hole, they cross and reform as an upside-down image. However simple this explanation, the physical properties of light were not understood at the time and the camera obscura was thought to be miraculous and supernatural.

Preserving an Image

By the nineteenth century, the camera obscura, known as a magic lantern, was found at seaside resorts and other scenic areas,

In 1826 Joseph Nicéphore Niépce took the first known photograph, pictured. At this time, it took between eight and ten hours to develop one photo.

where tourists would line up to peer into a box that held tiny color images of the majestic outdoor world. Around the same time, chemists were experimenting with various substances that would allow them to make a permanent record of the image cast inside a magic lantern. In France, a wealthy aristocrat, Joseph Nicéphore Niépce, became obsessed with the idea and experimented, unsuccessfully, with a variety of light-sensitive chemicals for more than a dozen years. Niépce tried silver salts, iron oxide, manganese, varnishes, and even tree sap coated onto sheets of copper, pewter, glass, and tin. Finally, in 1826, Niépce was able to take the first photograph, a picture of the courtyard of his country estate in the village of St. Loup-de-Varennes, taken from an upper window of his villa. The photo was taken with a camera obscura fitted with a polished pewter plate coated with an asphalt substance called bitumen of Judea. This sub-

In the mid-1800s, the work of Joseph Nicéphore Niépce and Louis-Jacques-Mandé Daguerre propelled the art of photography forward.

In order to properly exhibit these treasures, Stieglitz opened the Little Galleries of the Photo-Secession, the first private commercial gallery dedicated to photography. Located at 291 Fifth Avenue in New York, the gallery came to be known simply as "291." The first show, in November 1905, featured one hundred photos of members' work, for sale to art patrons and museum curators. In an effort to further cement the link between photography and art, 291 also held exhibitions by artistic masters such as Auguste Rodin, Henri Matisse, Pablo Picasso, and Georgia O'Keeffe (Stieglitz's wife).

A Move Toward Modernism

The 291 gallery closed in 1917 around the time *Camera Work* ceased publication. However, Stieglitz remained extremely influential in the world of photography, not only through his own work but also by promoting a new generation of photographers. By this time, Stieglitz had long abandoned his fondness for soft-focus, painterly photography in favor of a new, sharp-focus precision that came to be known as "straight" photography. This genre requires photographers to depict a scene as realistically as possible without the benefit of lens coatings, filters, or manipulation of the print in the darkroom. While this may sound like a return to the early days of photography, straight photographers created unusual, abstract photos featuring dark shadows, strong contrasts, and odd, disorienting camera positions.

Stieglitz promoted three photographers, Paul Strand, Charles Sheeler, and Morton Schamberg, known as the "Trinity of Photography," who defined the straight genre. Strand, in particular, was the leader of this movement, so much so that the

"Blind Woman, New York" by Paul Strand is an example of "straight" photography. This style depicts subjects as realistically as possible, without manipulation of any kind on the part of the photographer.

IMOGEN CUNNINGHAM

Imogen Cunningham's photos of plants and flowers, taken in the late 1920s and 1930s, epitomize the genre of straight photography when applied to images of nature. The following biography is taken from Imogen Cunningham: The Modernist Years *by Richard Lorenz:*

Imogen Cunningham [1906–1976] was the quintessential American woman photographer of the twentieth century and an artist whose expansive vision created many great icons of photographic history. . . . 1921 was a distinct turning point for Cunningham. She refined her vision of nature, changing her focus from the long to the near. Her interest in detailed pattern and form became evident in studies of bark texture and contorted tree trunks along the Carmel coast, a writhing snake curled on a gnarled Monterey cypress, and the trumpet-shaped morning glory that grew wild in her backyard. . . .

By 1923, Cunningham broke new ground in West Coast photography. . . . During 1923–25, Cunningham made an extended series of magnolia flower studies which became increasingly simplified as she sought to recognize the form within the object. Cunningham did not always photograph plant materials straightforwardly or in their natural habitats; her arrangements were often created spontaneously in a spirit of fun, albeit with a solid sense of design.

Richard Lorenz, *Imogen Cunningham: The Modernist Years*. Originally published Tokyo: Treville Company Ltd., 1993. Also available at www.imogencunningham.com/BIO/frameset_bio.html.

final two issues of *Camera Work* were filled exclusively with his photos. Stieglitz explained this unusual decision, writing of Strand, "The work is brutally direct. Devoid of flim-flam; devoid of trickery and any 'ism' [such as pictorialism]; devoid of any attempt to mystify an ignorant public, including the pho-

Glasgow, and Dresden. Photographers who exhibited at these annual shows aligned themselves with artists and sought, through their work, to differentiate themselves from photographic scientists, technicians, and amateurs. In New York City, the pictorialist movement was drawing even more attention due to the booming turn-of-the-century economy, which provided an economic incentive for photographers to hold regular exhibitions, establish private galleries, and publish magazines dedicated to pictorialism. The center of the movement was the New York Camera Club and its influential magazine *Camera Notes*, which was widely praised for its high-quality photo reproductions and original design. Award-winning photographer Alfred Stieglitz founded the magazine in 1897, but by the early 1900s, he felt restricted by the New York Camera Club, describing its members' work as "technically perfect, pictorially rotten."[15] Tired of working with those whose pictures he considered stale and orthodox, Stieglitz left the club in 1902 and formed the Photo-Secession movement. This group had an elite membership handpicked by Stieglitz, including Gertrude Käsebier, Edward Steichen, Alvin Langdon Coburn, and Clarence H. White.

To promote the Photo-Secession movement, Stieglitz established *Camera Work* magazine, a beautifully designed periodical printed on expensive Japanese rice paper. *Camera Work* is described by Bunnell:

> Not distracted by the underlying debate over whether photography should or should not be straightforward as opposed to manipulated, Stieglitz dealt instead with the notion of significant content, significant expression, and superior craft. . . .

"Spring Showers, New York" by Alfred Stieglitz is an example of work from the Photo-Secession movement.

Sumptuous almost beyond belief for a photographic journal, or even an art periodical . . . *Camera Work* was a forum for the display of quality illustrations. Significantly stressed in most of the magazine's issues was the fact that each reproduction was made from the original negative, and that it was printed to the highest standards available.[16]

While the production values of *Camera Work* were notable, the success of the magazine was due to the painterly photographs displayed on its pages. Stieglitz's photographs of New York street scenes, such as "Spring Showers" and "From the Back Window, 291," bring to mind the finest paintings of the French impressionists.

In addition to valuing artistic composition, Photo-Secessionists often created their photos as expensive platinum prints, a technique that takes its name from the salts in the platinum family of metals that are present in the light-sensitive emulsion that coats the paper. For example, Steichen's photo "The Flat Iron Building, Evening," was printed with platinum and an added blue tint. The photograph is a contrast in shadows, silhouettes, and blue, black, and gray tones. Steichen's fondness for the expensive platinum prints was based on their unique beauty and permanence, described by gallery owner John Stevenson:

The delicate, rich platinum tones range from warm black, to reddish brown, to expanded mid-tone grays that are unobtainable in silver prints. In the deepest shadows the platinum print still presents information; the platinum whites are delicate and the depth of the image is alive and three-dimensional. Platinum prints are not only exceptionally beautiful, they are among the most permanent objects invented by human beings! . . . Incredibly, a platinum image, properly made, can last thousands of years. It is as enduring as steel or stone and will even outlive the fine paper it is printed upon.[17]

A New Way to See the World

The pioneers of photography were artists, inventors, and entrepreneurs, and since the earliest days of the camera, photography has been almost equal parts business, science, and art. Louis-Jacques-Mandé Daguerre, who perfected the first photographic process, embraced all three fields of study. Born in France in 1787 (or 1789 according to some sources), Daguerre's early studies included architecture, physics, and theater design. He became a commercially successful artist when he combined his knowledge of these fields to become a painter of panoramas, which in their original form were large circular paintings that exhibited wide views of entire cities. First displayed in Scotland in 1792, panoramas were a major commercial success in Paris, where viewers paid large sums of money to stand at the center of the painting and admire the grand view provided by the artist.

Daguerre took the theatrical illusion one step further when, with the help of the camera obscura, he created the first diorama in 1822. Dioramas were constructed in specially designed buildings where up to 350 people sat on a large rotating floor. Huge pictures, up to 70 by 40 feet (21 by 12 m), were painted on both sides of a translucent material such as linen and illuminated with elaborate theatrical lighting. The front picture would be seen with direct lighting while various colors were revealed from the back of the painting by special lights in the rear.

Diorama production made Daguerre a rich man and allowed him to pursue another form of illusion, photography. After many experiments, he discovered that a photograph could be taken with a metal plate coated with light-sensitive silver halide particles. When he demonstrated his invention to some of France's most prominent scientists, politicians, and journalists, the theatrical designer and inventor was awarded a generous lifetime pension from the French government of 6,000 francs a year, roughly half a million U.S. dollars. In exchange for the money, Daguerre agreed to publish his method for creating a photographic plate, thereby granting all French citizens the right to use the daguerreotype process.

While Daguerre lived the remainder of his life in semi-obscurity, the use of his photographic process quickly spread

The first daguerreotype cameras were not only expensive, but also weighed more than 100 pounds (45kg).

As the first commercial portrait photographers in the world, Wolcott and Johnson quickly made large sums of money and moved their studio from Wolcott's living room to a larger space on the top floor of the Granite Building on

THE DAGUERREOTYPE PROCESS

This description of the painstaking daguerreotype process from A New History of Photography *makes clear that early photographers had to have scientific skills to take quality pictures:*

The photographic plate was made of copper, thinly plated on one side of the purest silver. . . .

1. Having been sprinkled with pumice, the plate was buffed with a soft cotton rag lightly soaked in olive oil. Then it was cleaned with diluted nitric acid and dried. . . .

2. The plate . . . was then placed face down inside a box containing iodine crystals. It was left there for 5 to 30 minutes, until the iodine vapor gave it a golden-yellow color which indicated that the sensitization process was complete. . . .

3. Within a period of an hour, in total darkness, the plate was placed in the camera, and the exposure was made: this varied from 3 to 30 minutes.

4. Still in total darkness, the plate was then placed face down in another box . . . over a small cup of mercury, which was heated to 60 degrees Celsius [140 degrees Fahrenheit]. The mercury vapor condensed on the plate, but only on those parts which had been exposed to light. . . .

5. The image was then fixed by immersing the plate in a solution of sea salt.

Michel Frizot, ed., *A New History of Photography*. Köln, Germany: Könemann, 1994, p. 38.

Broadway. To further enhance the use of reflected light, they cut a skylight in the roof of their new studio and built a circular sitting room that could be moved about on a small railway. These arrangements allowed them to photograph sitters in the best possible light as the sun moved across the sky.

The American Daguerreotype

Before long, Wolcott and Johnson's photographic monopoly fell to a host of competitors that grew every day. Daguerreotype studios opened in Boston and Philadelphia as well as in major cities in England, France, and Germany. Despite the competition, however, daguerreotypes remained expensive and studio owners went out of their way to cater to the needs of an upper-class clientele. Renowned photojournalist Timm Starl explains:

> What [the clients] wanted was a portrait which would display all their newly acquired refinement and dignity

ly recognized experts on nineteenth-century photography, write: "Always eager, inventive, and enterprising, Americans were ready to embark on any new venture which promised financial gain. . . . With few exceptions, Europe had no counterpart to this group of restless, inquisitive, Americans."[7]

New Processes

It was said in 1846 that every man, woman, and child in the United States had been photographed by a daguerreotypist. While this was probably an exaggeration, it shows the astounding popularity of what was one of the earliest fads in America. The popularity of photography spurred innovations and improvements in cameras, lenses, and the photographic method itself. However, one problem remained unsolved—the daguerreotype process created only a single, irreproducible picture while most people wanted multiple copies of their portraits. Some photographers provided a workable, if expensive, solution to the problem by lining up six cameras in a row to take a half dozen daguerreotypes at the same time. Other photographers ran a side business making copies simply by taking a picture of the original plate. However, these reproductions were high in contrast and showed a significant loss of detail and quality.

Although there was a great demand for a method that would allow infinite reproductions of a photo, most people were unaware of the calotype, developed in England in 1841 by William Henry Fox Talbot. The calotype process produced a paper negative that could be used to make numerous prints on specially treated paper. However, while Daguerre published exacting details of the daguerreotype process in manuals, Talbot was much more secretive about his invention, patenting his process and publishing only vague details. This secrecy prevented the public from learning about his method and using it freely. In addition, calotype exposures required thirty seconds to twenty minutes, which made the process impractical for portraiture, and the development process required several days to complete. This meant that sitters could not leave the studio with a photograph in hand.

Latticed Window
(with the Camera Obscura)
August 1835

When first made, the squares
of glass about 200 in number
could be counted, with help
of a lens.

William Henry Fox Talbot invented the photographic negative, which allows numerous prints of a photograph to be made. Pictured here is the first negative produced by Talbot.

The disadvantages of the calotype were extremely frustrating to London sculptor Frederick Scott Archer, who used the process to take pictures of his artwork. In 1847, Archer began tinkering with the calotype process and, like Daguerre, quickly abandoned the artistic profession in order to invent a better photographic method. Several years later, Archer had a breakthrough when he discovered what came to be called the wet-plate collodion process. This procedure begins with cotton that has been soaked in nitric acid. The cotton, now called guncotton for its explosive qualities, is then dissolved in ether and alcohol to produce a thick, syrupy liquid called a collodion. Light-sensitive potassium iodide salts are added to the collodion and the viscous mixture is applied to a piece of glass. After the ether and alcohol evaporate, the plate is placed in a bath of silver nitrate, which produces a "wet plate" ready for exposure in the camera. (If the plate dries before exposure, it is unusable.) After exposure, the plate is taken to a darkroom and processed with chemicals that leave behind a solid glass negative that can be used to produce multiple images on chemically treated photographic paper.

Hanna Höch combined her own personal photos, images cut from magazines, small pieces of metal machinery, and other objects in order to produce large pictures in a genre called photo-collage. Höch was considered a political radical, and her collages often used humor and absurdity to satirize the political atmosphere in Germany and the treatment of women before World War II.

PHOTOGRAPHY: ART'S MORTAL ENEMY

In the early years of photography, many critics were hostile to the use of the camera in the world of art. The father of modern art criticism, Charles Baudelaire, was among those who lamented that art itself was being destroyed by photography, as the following 1859 article makes clear:

As the photographic industry was the refuge of every would-be painter, every painter too ill-endowed or too lazy to complete his studies, this universal infatuation [with photography] bore not only the mark of a blindness, an imbecility, but had also the air of a vengeance. I do not believe, or at least I do not wish to believe, in the absolute success of such a brutish conspiracy, in which, as in all others, one finds both fools and knaves; but I am convinced that the ill-applied developments of photography, like all other purely material developments of progress, have contributed much to the impoverishment of the French artistic genius, which is already so scarce. . . . [It is] obvious that this industry, by invading the territories of art, has become art's most mortal enemy. . . . If photography is allowed to supplement art in some of its functions, it will soon have supplanted or corrupted it altogether, thanks to the stupidity of the multitude which is [photography's] natural ally.

Charles Baudelaire, "On Photography, from The Salon of 1859," California State University at Sacramento, 2006. www.csus.edu/indiv/o/obriene/art109/readings/11%20Baudelaire%20Photography.htm.

Group f/64

While Höch and Ray were at the peak of their creative powers, fine art photographers in California could not have been more isolated from Europe both culturally and geographically. It is little wonder then that an entirely different school of fine art photography developed in San Francisco, beginning in the early 1930s. This genre was dedicated to capturing nature's grandeur, free from photographic tricks and artistic fads. At the center of this movement were the photographers known as Group f/64: Ansel Adams, Imogen Cunningham, Consuelo Kanaga, Sonya Noskowiak, and Edward Weston. The term *f/64* refers to the smallest aperture setting on a large-format camera. Photographs taken with this lens setting have a maximum depth of field, meaning they are sharp and clear from foreground to background.

The idea for Group f/64 began in 1930 when Adams met Paul Strand at a party. Impressed with Strand's seriousness and dedication to straight photography, Adams decided to pursue his own vision of realism, using the spectacular mountains, rivers, and forests of the western United States as his subjects. Two years later, he founded Group f/64 and wrote a manifesto for the group that leaves little doubt about his negative feeling concerning cubism, surrealism, and photomontage: "The members of Group f/64 believe that photography, as an art form, must develop along lines defined by the actualities and limitations of the photographic medium, and must always remain independent of ideological conventions of art."[23]

The West Coast group held frequent exhibitions that gained Adams widespread recognition as a premier nature photographer. At a time when the West was largely unsettled, Adams used pack animals to carry his large-format 8 x 10 view cameras, several lenses, tripods, and film holders to isolated wilderness areas in California, Wyoming, and elsewhere. The large negatives produced by his camera created stunningly detailed prints that remain among the most beloved images ever taken of natural wonders such as Half Dome, El Capitan, and Bridal Veil Falls in Yosemite National Park. His photos were also used to

Ansel Adams is one of the most well-known nature photographers of all time. Pictured opposite is his work "El Capitan, Winter, Yosemite National Park, California, 1948."

tographers themselves. These photographs are the direct expression of today."[18]

That expression was based on the art movement known as cubism, a style created by Pablo Picasso, Georges Braque, and Paul Cézanne. These cubist painters reduced their subjects to geometric forms and depicted them from multiple vantage points. Cubism in photography is epitomized by Strand's unique abstractions taken on a porch in Connecticut in 1915 and 1916, described by *New York Times* photo critic Andy Grundberg: "In these pictures, the camera is tilted radically, reducing the recognizability of the porch and eliminating any reference to the horizontal. A lattice-work of shadows defines the picture space. The images are freed from gravity and allowed to exist independently of what they depict."[19]

"Unrestrained, Convulsive Beauty"

Cubism was among many artistic "isms" that would influence photography in the following years. Another European style, surrealism, also had a profound effect on fine art photography. Surrealists looked beyond reality in an attempt to create images previously seen only in dreams or hallucinations. According to an essay on the Metropolitan Museum of Art Web site:

> The Surrealists did not rely on reasoned analysis or sober calculation; on the contrary, they saw the forces of reason blocking the access routes to the imagination. Their efforts to tap the creative powers of the unconscious set [them] on a path that carried them through the territory of dreams, intoxication, chance, sexual ecstasy, and madness. The images obtained by such means . . . were prized precisely to the degree that they captured these moments of psychic intensity in provocative forms of unrestrained, convulsive beauty.[20]

The leading proponent of surrealist photography was Brooklyn native Man Ray, who learned how to take photos in

1915 only to document his artwork. Discussing this career move, Ray said, "If I'd had the nerve, I'd have become a thief or a gangster [to support my painting] but since I didn't, I became a photographer."[21] Whatever the case, Ray's artwork led him to a friendship with French artist Marcel Duchamp, who took him to Paris and introduced him to an elite group of writers and artists including Picasso, Ernest Hemingway, Gertrude Stein, and Salvador Dali. Temporarily putting his artistic career aside, Ray opened a commercial photography studio to take photographs of his famous friends.

Ray's girlfriend, Alice Prin, known as Kiki, became his favorite model, and he took a series of portraits of her that remain among the classic surrealistic works of that era. In one photo, a close-up of Kiki's eye was photographed with small glass tears beneath it; in another, she is seen sitting nude from behind with the gracefully shaped sound holes of a violin painted on her back. However, Ray's most famous photographs happened quite by accident. One day while he was working in the darkroom, a sheet of unexposed paper fell into the developing tray. Rather than throw it out, Ray placed a small glass funnel, a beaker, and a darkroom thermometer on it and exposed it to light. When he finished developing it, Ray unexpectedly had a photograph that depicted the silhouettes of the objects. In later experiments, Ray made similar pictures of objects such as a key, wire mesh, paper scraps, and even a pistol. He called his new style of photographs Rayographs, and they became an instant sensation among the Parisian surrealists. Today Rayographs, along with Ray's other pictures, are considered classic representations of a style that permanently changed the rules of photography. As David Travis explains in *On the Art of Fixing a Shadow:* "The Rayograph freed photography from being defined by camera images alone and reduced the definition of the medium to the registration of light. The technique separated what went on in front of the camera from what happened on the chemically prepared surface inside."[22]

Rayograms were but one manifestation of photographic expression that was not dependent upon the camera. In Berlin,

and also the status they occupied in the social hierarchy. Very soon after the first studios opened, it became the norm for them to be furnished as a domestic interior, so that the sitter could show off both the material means and the education they possessed. A painted background, expensive-looking furniture, and various accessories, almost always including a book, formed the setting in which the sitter took up their pose.[4]

Like many new technologies, daguerreotypes were first popularized by customers who could afford to pay for the pricey and exotic new process. The potential profits attracted throngs of entrepreneurs eager to get into the business, and the competition eventually lowered prices, making the once-expensive techniques available to almost everyone. By 1846, there were twenty daguerreotype studios in New York alone; by 1851 there were over seventy. Thanks to this explosive growth, the price of the daguerreotype fell to about one dollar, and studios were able to produce the portraits rapidly. British photographer and author Peter Marshall discusses this phenomenon on the About Photography Web site:

> The daguerreotype was ideally suited to use by professional portraitists in their photo studios, where they had well-equipped and organized workshops for preparing and processing the plates. Their great success in America and in particular the high technical quality of the best work there—the term "American Daguerreotype" was used as a byword for quality—was largely due to the use of mechanical methods of plate polishing and preparation in a highly controlled manner, an early application of mass production techniques.[5]

Traveling Daguerreotypists

Despite the quality control offered in a studio setting, Americans of the day were also great wanderers. It was not long before hundreds of traveling photographers, called daguerreotypists, took to the road. These itinerate craftsmen, many of them former portrait painters who became unemployed after the camera was invented, traipsed across the countryside with their heavy cameras strapped to their backs.

To drum up business, daguerreotypists would print up handbills to announce their arrival and rent a room on a town's main street to serve as a studio. One such photographer, Edwin Foot, distributed the following handbill in Montrose, Pennsylvania, in 1842:

Mr. Edwin Foot, would respectfully announce to the Gentlemen and Ladies of Montrose and vicinity that he is prepared to take Daguerreotype miniatures in good style. Persons desirous of obtaining an exact likeness of their features, indelibly set on silver, put into elegant morocco [leather] cases, and for a trifle too, hardly worth mentioning, will do well to call on the subscriber who may be found for a few days in the corner room over Wm. L. Post & Co.'s Store. Hours of attendance from ten A.M. till half past four P.M. He will also give instructions to a limited number of young men in this beautiful and highly interesting art.[6]

In this manner Foot was able not only to sell daguerreotypes for a small sum, or "trifle," but to earn money and create even more daguerreotypists with his instructions to young men. This was a uniquely American trend, as Floyd and Marion Rinhart, international-

PHOTOGRAPHIC FACTORIES

The wet-plate collodion system allowed photography to become an industrialized process, by which thousands of prints from a single negative could be made and sold to the public. In On the Art of Fixing a Shadow, *Joel Snyder describes the commercialization of the photography business:*

Since collodion negatives could be printed quickly and easily by relatively unskilled workers, they offered the opportunity for the production of immense numbers of cheap prints. This led, in turn, to a division of labor within the photographic studios in which one or two skilled managers directed the activities of many unskilled printers. And it was this division of labor that brought photography into the rapidly evolving industrial culture of the nineteenth century. It became possible for travel and architectural photographers to produce tens of thousands of inexpensive prints and stereographic cards a month—some firms employed three or four hundred low-salaried workers, whose sole job was to produce prints for sale to the public. The wet collodion negative introduced photographic prints into popular culture.

Sarah Greenough, Joel Snyder, David Travis, and Colin Westerbeck, *On the Art of Fixing a Shadow.* Boston: Bulfinch, 1989, pp. 21–22.

take a number of portraits, usually eight to twelve, on a single negative. By allowing a large number of prints to be made from a single plate, Disdéri's process lowered the price of portraiture and made it even easier for photo factories to produce large numbers of a single shot. For example, the picture of Napoleon was reproduced more than one hundred thousand times within a few months.

The desire for *cartes-de-visite* pictures of well-known figures was not limited to France. In England, more than one hundred thousand people purchased portraits of Queen Victoria, Prince Albert, and other members of the royal family. In the United States, a portrait of President Abraham Lincoln taken in 1860 sold over two hundred thousand copies. These figures created a surge in the number of studios. In London, the twelve studios open in 1851 were rivaled by more than two hundred in 1860. By that time in Paris, over thirty-three thousand people worked directly in the photo industry.

The *cartes-de-visite* also gave rise to the family portrait album. Unlike a daguerreotype that was mounted on the wall like an expensive painting, the new, cheap portraits could be glued into books with dozens of other pictures, not only of family members, but opera singers, actors, and poets.

Today, the gallery of portraits from the early years of photography provides a window into a world both foreign and familiar. The clothing, hairstyles, and serious expressions show a bygone era sharply different from the modern world. But the faces and poses also reveal a common humanity that remains unchanged through the passing centuries. And this is the fascination with photography that was recognized almost instantly when the first daguerreotypes appeared—the camera captures and preserves a single moment in time long after the person in the picture has passed away.

Archer shared the wet-plate method with the public in February 1851, publishing the results of his experiments in an article, "On the Use of Collodion in Photography," in *Chemist* magazine. The wet-plate process was quickly recognized as superior, faster, and cheaper than the daguerreotype. In addition, the collodion process allowed a picture to be developed in what was then considered a very short exposure time of three seconds. This allowed photographers, for the first time, to take pictures of fleeting events such as water rippling, waves breaking, smoke rising, and clouds billowing across the sky.

A "wet plate" that has gone through the collodion process. While wet, it is ready for exposure in the camera.

Presenting the World

Archer never patented his photographic invention and died penniless six years after his discovery. By the time of his death, however, the wet-plate system had almost universally replaced the daguerreotype, ushering in a new era of photography. Gone were the tiny, precious portraits of individuals wrapped in velvet. In their place were large, high-quality, inexpensive paper prints, many of which presented the most astounding scenery the world had to offer.

FREDERICK SCOTT ARCHER

Frederick Scott Archer invented the wet-plate collodion process that was used by photographers from 1851 to 1880. The following short biography on the Edin Photo Web site provides details of Archer's life:

[Frederick] Scott Archer allowed the process to be used free of copyright [and] made no wealth from his discovery. He received little recognition in his lifetime for his discovery, and attempts amongst photographers to obtain a pension for him in his ill health were unsuccessful. He died in poverty at the age of 44, six years after publishing his discovery.

The Photographic Society of Scotland announced [his death] at its Meeting on 8 June 1857:

> A subscription has been opened among Members of the Society in aid of the Widow and Family of the late Mr. Scott Archer, the introducer of the Collodion Process, who have been left completely destitute by his recent death. It is important that the sum collected be forwarded to London immediately.

Edin Photo, "Early Photographic Process—Wet Collodion," 2006. www.edinphoto.org.uk/1_early/1_early_photography_-_processes_-_wet_collodion.htm.

stance is unusual in that it hardens in light, leaving an image after an eight- to ten-hour exposure to sunlight.

After Niépce's initial discovery, he worked for years to reduce the long exposure times. After his death in 1833, his work was carried on by his partner, a Parisian artist and theatrical designer named Louis-Jacques-Mandé Daguerre. In 1839, Daguerre coated a mirror-polished plate with photosensitive silver halide particles and exposed it to an image for ten to twenty minutes. The result was a photograph that the inventor called a daguerreotype.

The daguerreotype was imperfect in its early incarnation. The long exposure times made it suitable only to take pictures of buildings or still lifes. However, by the 1840s, improvements in lenses and chemical formulas reduced exposure times to a few seconds. With these new processes, the modest camera obscura, combined with metal plates and a few chemicals, began to remake art and society much the way television or the Internet did in the following century. For the first time, people of modest means could preserve their images for future generations without paying a large fee to an artist.

An Ongoing Photography Craze

Photography became even more accessible to the general public in 1888 when Eastman invented flexible, dry roll film that fit inside the simple Kodak camera. After the film was exposed by the photographer, it was sent to a lab to be developed. With the slogan "You press the button, we do the rest,"[2] the Eastman Kodak company made photography accessible to nearly everyone. A further photographic revolution began in 1900 with Kodak's introduction of the six-exposure Brownie camera. Kodak sold 150,000 Brownies—at a dollar each—the first year. During the seventy-five years that followed, millions of Brownies were sold. These simple box cameras could be operated even by young children, and many famous photographers, including Ansel Adams and Dorothy Armstrong, fondly remembered taking their first photographs with a Brownie.

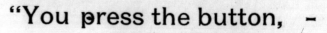
The invention of the simple Kodak camera in 1888 made photography affordable and accessible to the public.

The Brownie spawned an amateur photography craze that has barely subsided to this day. In the 1960s, the simple Brownie was largely replaced by the 35mm single-lens reflex (SLR) camera. Like the Brownie, the SLR is nearly foolproof, but it is a much more complex instrument, capable of taking the simplest snapshots or stunning fine art prints.

In the ever-changing world of photographic technology, the SLR has now become obsolete since the introduction of the digital camera in the 1990s. Digitals have the best features of the SLR but have eliminated the need for film. The quest to capture images on a chemically coated surface that dominated the lives of so many nineteenth-century inventors has been eliminated by the digital revolution. What has not changed is the human fascination with light, imagery, and artistry. And as long as people wish to communicate their thoughts and feelings through photographs, the magical lanterns of the modern age will remain as important in the twenty-first century as they were in the 1840s.

A Fine Art Movement

The first two decades of photography were marked by rapid commercialization, first of the daguerreotype process and then of the wet-plate collodion system that replaced it. Driven by the public's fascination with portraits and travel pictures, photographers produced millions of photos while fueling a lucrative new industry. However, not everyone bowed to the commercialism that required photographers to satisfy the often uninspired demands of their customers. Away from the bustling portrait studios and photographic factories, a new class of artist was using the camera to express creative photographic visions. These were reproduced in small numbers and marketed as high-quality prints to dealers, collectors, and museum curators.

Elevating Photography to Art

In the earliest days of photography, the accepted forms of fine art consisted of heroic paintings of emperors, mythical scenes taken from great literature, and depictions of the natural world that inspired joy and hopefulness. Moved by these masterworks, a select group of photographers spent considerable time and effort staging photographs and developing them into museum-quality works that would withstand the test of time.

In England, the celebrated and influential photographer Roger Fenton began his career as a painter, studying art in France before showing his work in annual exhibitions at the respected Royal Academy. Fenton is best known for his photographs of the Crimean War in 1854. However, in later years he drew on his knowledge of art and composition to create museum-quality still lifes and scenes featuring costumed models in historical settings, known by the French term *tableaux vivants*, or "living pictures."

Fenton's tableaux photographs from his 1859 Orientalist series demonstrate that photographers can represent artistic visions in a painterly manner. To create these pictures, Fenton posed professional models and friends in Turkish robes and turbans sitting cross-legged on rugs, pouring coffee, smoking water pipes, or playing exotic instruments. The resulting fifty photos were not historical representations of a culture but rather costume dramas meant to evoke escapist feelings of fantasy and mystery.

Fenton based the Orientalist series on paintings by famous French artists such as Eugène Delacroix. In doing so he was hoping to elevate the status of photography to the dignity of fine art. Creating art with a camera, however, was a difficult and time-consuming task that required a talent for painting. Early fine art photographers first had to create hand-drawn sketches of their tableaux. To create a scene, backdrops needed to be painted, costumes sewn, props built, and exposures carefully formulated. Such an effort could take weeks or even months.

At the height of the tableaux trend in the late 1850s and 1860s, photographers used their pictures to tell stories or present moral lessons. This was done through a technique called combination printing, in which several negatives were used to create a single picture. This process was first seen in England in 1857, when Swedish-born artist and photographer Oscar Rejlander created an incredibly elaborate photo, "The Two Ways of Life." This photograph, like many paintings at the time, was created to demonstrate moral lessons popular during the reign of Queen Victoria. It is described by art historian and former cura-

tor for the International Center of Photography in New York, Anne H. Hoy:

> ["The Two Ways of Life"] is a catalog of poses and of Victorian definitions of virtue and vice. The photographer made over 30 negatives to illustrate industry and dissipation, using 28 models from a troupe specializing in tableaux vivants. Scantily and classically draped models presented vignettes of gambling, sloth, and debauchery on the left, of piety, charity to the sick, and manual labor on the right. . . . The intended instruction and moral uplift of the photograph commended it to Victorians, who expected art to aid self-improvement.[9]

Rejlander taught his combination photo technique to another art photographer, Henry Peach Robinson, who earned the nickname "king of photographic picture making" for his perfection of the method. Robinson's most famous picture, "Fading Away" (1858), is made from five negatives. The picture, which closely resembles a fine oil painting, shows a young girl dying of tuberculosis, surrounded by distraught family members. Her father stares out the window at banks of moody clouds in the sky.

Oscar Rejlander pieced together thirty negatives to create the look of a painting for his 1857 photograph "The Two Ways of Life."

Henry Peach Robinson's most famous photograph, "Fading Away," was made by combining five negatives.

At the time of its creation, most people thought "Fading Away" was a photograph of an actual family, not a composite using models. This made the photograph quite controversial as some felt that the subject was too personal and painful to be depicted in a photograph. As Robert Leggat, fellow of the Royal Photographic Society in London, writes, "It would seem that it was perfectly in order for painters to paint pictures on such themes, but not for photographers to do so."[10] To quell the controversy, Robinson described how he had created the combination print, but this explanation only intensified the criticism as people then felt that their emotions had been manipulated by photographic tricks. In explaining himself, Robinson stated, "Any dodge, trick and conjuration of any kind is open to the photographer's use. . . . It is his imperative duty to avoid the mean, the base and the ugly, and to aim to elevate his subject . . . and to correct the unpicturesque. . . . A great deal can be done and very beautiful pictures made, by a mixture of the real and the artificial in a picture."[11]

A Means of Self-Expression

The art of photography would become much more controversial in the late 1870s with the introduction of a revolutionary new method called the gelatin dry-plate process. This new method was discovered in 1871 by English physician Richard Leach Maddox, who found that photographic chemicals could be coated on a glass plate using a gelatin emulsion, which was then allowed to dry. Compared to wet collodion, the advantages to this process, perfected in 1878, were many. Dry plates could be prepared in advance and stored for long periods of time after exposure. This freed the photographer in the field from the laborious process of making the plate, developing it before it dried, and then coating the next plate for exposure. Dry plates also allowed exposure times of 1/25 of a second, an amazing improvement that allowed photographers to take stop-action pictures of a horse galloping in a field or a man in midair jumping across a crevasse. Faster exposure times also freed photographers from the heavy tripod and allowed spontaneous photographs to be taken with small, handheld cameras.

The improvements provided by the dry gelatin method created a photographic revolution. In 1888, George Eastman developed compact, easy-to-handle roll film in which the gelatin emulsion was coated on a flexible strip of celluloid. Now it was possible for a wide segment of society to own not only photographs but cameras as well. This changed the entire nature of the art of photography, as Sarah Greenough, head of the Department of Photographs at the National Gallery of Art in Washington, D.C., writes:

> The legions of hand camera enthusiasts created new subjects, new criteria of pictorial structure and function. . . . In doing so they shook the very core of the medium, challenging rules and assumptions that had been evolving for the past fifty years. . . . For many it was a delightful way to record intimate scenes of friends and family; for others it was a tool enlisted in personal crusades to document social conditions or

dying cultures; and for still others it became a means of self-expression.[12]

Impressionism and Pictorialism

As photography came to be dominated by amateurs, the mystery and wonder of the photographic arts quickly faded. Since even a child could wield a Brownie camera to take high-quality pictures of family members, photography studios became unnecessary. Thousands went bankrupt in the 1880s and 1890s. However, some professional photographers sought to preserve their vocation by defining their work as artistic in nature and beyond the abilities of what they called the backyard Brownie snapshooters.

During this era, the most popular style of art was the impressionism of painters Claude Monet, Pierre-Auguste

The style of photography known as pictorialism required photographers to produce soft-focus pictures, which depicted objects blurred around the edges.

torted in agonized expressions. Initially, critics and the public condemned the painting as an incoherent hodgepodge, but the work soon came to be seen as a powerful antiwar statement and remains an iconic symbol of the violence and terror that dominated world events during the remainder of the twentieth century.

The impulse to create art—whether painting animals with crude pigments on a cave wall, sculpting a human form from marble, or commemorating human tragedy in a mural—thus serves many purposes. It offers an entertaining diversion, nourishes the imagination and the spirit, decorates and beautifies the world, and chronicles the age. But underlying all these functions is the desire to reveal that which is obscure—to illuminate, clarify, and perhaps ennoble. As Picasso himself stated, "The purpose of art is washing the dust of daily life off our souls."

The Eye on Art series is intended to assist readers in understanding the various roles of art in society. Each volume offers an in-depth exploration of a major artistic movement, medium, figure, or profession. All books in the series are beautifully illustrated with full-color photographs and diagrams. Riveting narrative, clear technical explanation, informative sidebars, fully documented quotes, a bibliography, and a thorough index all provide excellent starting points for research and discussion. With these features, the Eye on Art series is a useful introduction to the world of art—a world that can offer both insight and inspiration.

Introduction

A Rich History

Mention the word photography and many people think of digital cameras, cell phone cameras, or popular software programs that allow users to manipulate digital images. While these twenty-first-century tools characterize photography today, they are only the latest facets of a long tradition that combines science, artistry, history, and culture.

Although digital cameras utilize the latest technology, they perform the same task that the first cameras achieved in the 1820s—they record the light reflected off objects and turn it into photographic imagery. Digital cameras record light onto a computer chip while older cameras preserve it on film, but all photography depends on the manipulation of light. In fact, the word photography is derived from two Greek words, *photos*, or "light," and *graphos*, or "drawing." Photography literally means "light writing" or "writing with light." As George Eastman, the inventor of roll film and founder of Eastman Kodak Company, so eloquently stated, "Light makes photography. Embrace light. Admire it. Love it. But above all, know light. Know it for all you are worth, and you will know the key to photography."[1]

The idea that light projects images onto a surface was understood more than 2,500 years ago by Chinese philosopher Mo Ti, who invented what would later be called the camera

PHOTOGRAPHY

by Stuart A. Kallen

LUCENT BOOKS

An imprint of Thomson Gale, a part of The Thomson Corporation

Detroit • New York • San Francisco • New Haven, Conn. • Waterville, Maine • London

LIBRARY OF CONGRESS CATALOGING-IN-PUBLICATION DATA

Kallen, Stuart A., 1955–
  Photography / by Stuart A. Kallen.
    p. cm. — (Eye on art)
  Includes bibliographical references and index.
  ISBN 978-1-59018-986-3 (hardcover)
  1. Photography, Artistic. I. Title.
TR642.K34 2007
770—dc22

                                                              2007015978

ISBN-10:1-59018-986-8
Printed in the United States of America

The photographer who most exemplified the changes wrought by the wet-plate revolution was Francis Frith, an English photographer who owned a daguerreotype portrait studio in Liverpool. In 1856, after learning of the wet-plate system, Frith shut down his studio and took the first of three expeditions to Egypt and Palestine, where he photographed the Great Pyramid, holy sites, and other ancient monuments. Frith worked with very large cameras, 16 by 20 inches (40 by 50 cm), and managed against the odds to create stunning photographs with collodion in the hot, dusty desert. By 1859, Frith had published seven wildly successful books filled with his original prints. The next year he founded F. Frith & Co., a photography factory that printed postcards of his negatives and those of hundreds of other collodion photographers who worked for him, traveling throughout Asia, Europe, the Middle East, and elsewhere. Closer to home, Frith was inspired to photograph every town and village in Great Britain, paying close attention to

Photographer Francis Frith developed this 1858 photo, "Pyramids of El-Geezeh from the Southwest," using the wet-plate collodion method. The shorter exposure time gave photographers the freedom to move out of the portrait studio and photograph the world around them.

historical sites and areas of natural beauty. Within a few years, Frith & Co. postcards were sold in more than two thousand shops in Great Britain. Today the company Frith founded nearly 150 years ago has an Internet Web site (www.francisfrith.com) with 365,000 photographs, taken between 1860 and 1970, of 7,000 towns and villages throughout Britain.

Photographers like those who worked for Frith traveled with photography systems that easily rivaled the daguerreotypes in weight and bulk. Wet plates had to be developed in total darkness immediately after exposure, requiring the photographer to carry a heavy, black canvas tent. A wooden box, which also served as a table, contained a dozen flasks of chemicals, a jug of distilled water, basins, and the heavy glass plates used for negatives. The camera itself weighed more than 25 pounds (11kg), and a heavy tripod was needed to hold it during photo sessions.

Photographers moved this mass of equipment in various ways. Those traveling light fastened the 100 pounds (45kg) of gear onto their backs with thick leather straps. However, those who wanted to take several hundred pictures on their journey used mules and porters to carry the load. For example, when photographer Carleton Watkins traveled to the American West, he required a wagon and twelve mules to transport his equipment. Commenting on the difficulty of shooting hundreds of pictures in a pristine mountain valley, Watkins said, "The camera was a heavy enough load to carry to the top of the rocks, but that proved nothing in comparison with the chemicals and the boxes of plates—which in turned seemed light as a feather next to what seemed like a portable organ but was in fact the darkroom."[8]

Stereo Photographs

Despite the hardships encountered, photographers like Watkins were able to make their journeys pay handsomely. Pictures of natural and ancient wonders were in high demand and the rapid commercialization of photography was occurring on several fronts. One of the biggest crazes of the day was the stereo pho-

CONTENTS

Foreword

"Art has no other purpose than to brush aside . . . everything that veils reality from us in order to bring us face to face with reality itself."
—French philosopher Henri-Louis Bergson

Some thirty-one thousand years ago, early humans painted strikingly sophisticated images of horses, bison, rhinoceroses, bears, and other animals on the walls of a cave in southern France. The meaning of these elaborate pictures is unknown, although some experts speculate that they held ceremonial significance. Regardless of their intended purpose, the Chauvet-Pont-d'Arc cave paintings represent some of the first known expressions of the artistic impulse.

From the Paleolithic era to the present day, human beings have continued to create works of visual art. Artists have developed painting, drawing, sculpture, engraving, and many other techniques to produce visual representations of landscapes, the human form, religious and historical events, and countless other subjects. The artistic impulse also finds expression in glass, jewelry, and new forms inspired by new technology. Indeed, judging by humanity's prolific artistic output throughout history, one must conclude that the compulsion to produce art is an inherent aspect of being human, and the results are among humanity's greatest cultural achievements: masterpieces such as the architectural marvels of ancient Greece, Michelangelo's perfectly rendered statue *David*, Vincent van Gogh's visionary painting *Starry Night*, and endless other treasures.

The creative impulse serves many purposes for society. At its most basic level, art is a form of entertainment or the means for a satisfying or pleasant aesthetic experience. But art's true power lies not in its potential to entertain and delight but in its ability to enlighten, to reveal the truth, and by doing so to uplift the human spirit and transform the human race.

One of the primary functions of art has been to serve religion. For most of Western history, for example, artists were paid by the church to produce works with religious themes and subjects. Art was thus a tool to help human beings transcend mundane, secular reality and achieve spiritual enlightenment. One of the best-known, and largest-scale, examples of Christian religious art is the Sistine Chapel in the Vatican in Rome. In 1508 Pope Julius II commissioned Italian Renaissance artist Michelangelo to paint the chapel's vaulted ceiling, an area of 640 square yards (535 sq. m). Michelangelo spent four years on scaffolding, his neck craned, creating a panoramic fresco of some three hundred human figures. His paintings depict Old Testament prophets and heroes, sibyls of Greek mythology, and nine scenes from the Book of Genesis, including the Creation of Adam, the Fall of Adam and Eve from the Garden of Eden, and the Flood. The ceiling of the Sistine Chapel is considered one of the greatest works of Western art and has inspired the awe of countless Christian pilgrims and other religious seekers. As eighteenth-century German poet and author Johann Wolfgang von Goethe wrote, "Until you have seen this Sistine Chapel, you can have no adequate conception of what man is capable of."

In addition to inspiring religious fervor, art can serve as a force for social change. Artists are among the visionaries of any culture. As such, they often perceive injustice and wrongdoing and confront others by reflecting what they see in their work. One classic example of art as social commentary was created in May 1937, during the brutal Spanish civil war. On May 1 Spanish artist Pablo Picasso learned of the recent attack on the small Basque village of Guernica by German airplanes allied with fascist forces led by Francisco Franco. The German pilots had used the village for target practice, a three-hour bombing that killed sixteen hundred civilians. Picasso, living in Paris, channeled his outrage over the massacre into his painting *Guernica,* a black, white, and gray mural that depicts dismembered animals and fractured human figures whose faces are con-

tograph, which consists of two pictures taken with a stereoscopic camera, which has two lenses a few inches apart. One photograph is taken as the left eye sees the view and the other picture is slightly offset as the right eye would see it. The two photographs are mounted on a single card and viewed through a stereoscope, a device that gives the viewer the optical illusion of a three-dimensional vision of the scene.

The stereo photograph was as amazing to nineteenth-century viewers as the first televisions were to viewers a century later. In England, the London Stereoscopic Company, founded in 1854, become one of the biggest photographic publishing houses in the world. Its owner, George Swan Nottage, amassed a fortune selling stereo photos and eventually became the lord mayor of London. In Scotland, George Washington Wilson's printing works rivaled those in London. Wilson used the sunlight to expose the prints. His facilities, covering half an acre, contained racks of negative holders mounted on tables with wheels. These were rolled out into the sun on nice days or wheeled under a huge glass roof to make prints when it rained.

The same process was used to print pictures for photographic books, which were also extremely popular. During this era, before the photographic halftone printing process was invented,

A woman views images through a stereoscope, a device that gives the viewer the optical illusion of a three-dimensional image of the scene.

each book contained hand-developed photos that were meticulously glued into the pages.

Whatever form the photographs took, the wet-plate era was the first time that people could see detailed, accurate representations of the Parthenon in Greece, the Rocky Mountains in Colorado, the Nile River in Egypt, and thousands of other spectacles. At a time when most people rarely traveled more than a few days' horseback ride from home, these pictures brought the world to their doorsteps.

The Photo Card Fad

If there was any competition for these pictures of the scenic wonders of the world, it was photos of the rich, famous, and royal, whose pictures were in even greater demand. The demand for such photos spiked in 1860, when it became fashionable for actors, actresses, artists, philosophers, and statesmen to have their portraits taken in plush, lavishly decorated studios located in the most fashionable districts. When copies of the photos were displayed in studio windows, large crowds gathered on the street to gaze at the portraits. It was only a matter of time before studio owners began selling copies of prints to a portrait-hungry population.

Unlike the large pictures of scenery and ancient wonders, the portraits were sold in a small format called *cartes-de-visite*, or calling cards, that consisted of a photo mounted on a card sized 2.5 by 4 inches (6 by 10 cm). The *cartes-de-visite* craze was touched off by Emperor Napoleon III, who stopped off on his way to an invasion of Italy to have his portrait taken by Parisian photographer André Disdéri. The photographer had patented a process that allowed him to

Calling cards, or *cartes-de-visite*, were extremely popular in the mid- to late-1800s. Pictured here is a page from an 1865 photo album mounted with four *cartes-de-visite* portraits.

help preserve and protect the wilderness—the photos Adams took of the Kings River region of the Sierra Nevada in California inspired President Franklin Roosevelt to create Kings Canyon National Park in 1940.

While Adams dedicated his life to nature, other fine art photographers used their cameras to mock conventional society or document city life through an impressionistic lens. Whatever the final product, the fine art photographers in the first half of the twentieth century changed the course of photography. And they inspired millions of amateurs and professionals alike to photograph the world in novel and exhilarating ways.

3

Capturing the Human Drama

From the earliest days of photography, the camera was recognized as a unique tool for its ability to record facts and document history. The first photographic subjects included plants and flowers, city views, and buildings under construction. And the formal portraits of the mid-nineteenth century have come to serve as significant visual reminders of the fashions, activities, and attitudes of a bygone age.

Because the wonders of photography were largely enjoyed by the upper classes in the early days, only a few photographers considered using the camera to record the harsh, the unpleasant, and the ugly aspects of life. There was no shortage of misery in the nineteenth century, however, and almost as soon as the daguerreotype was invented, the camera was sent to record the battlefields of the Crimean War in Russia. Because of the long exposure times required by primitive cameras, photographers could only document battlefields littered with dead after combat was over.

It was not until the 1880s, when small, handheld cameras were introduced, that photographers started to record the harsh realities of the human drama that were largely invisible to mainstream culture. They took pictures of floods, fires, starving children, homeless people, and the residents of cramped, squalid apartments called tenements. These documents of disaster and injustice appeared around the time that the halftone printing process was refined. This method of printing photographs allowed social crusaders, for the first time, to publish their photographs in books, newspapers, and magazines. In fact, the first photo ever published in a newspaper depicted the shanty of a street person living in New York's Central Park.

The Mean Streets of the City

In the last quarter of the nineteenth century, New York City was one of the most densely populated places on earth, rife with crime, disease, starvation, and gang violence. Millions of recent immigrants from Europe worked fifteen-hour days in factories and packed into filthy wooden tenement buildings at night. Among those teeming masses was Jacob Riis, one of fifteen children in a Danish family that had immigrated in 1870.

Jacob Riis used his photography to document the plight of the poor in and around New York City in the late 1800s.

In 1877, at the age of twenty-eight, Riis went to work as a police reporter for the *New York Tribune.* His beat was the Mulberry Street police headquarters, a district infamous for its rotting slums and rickety tenements. Riis did not simply report the news, however, but used the written word to fight the injustices he saw every day. In 1887, Riis read about the invention of the magnesium flash, a method for taking photographs in low light using a tray full of explosive magnesium powder that the photographer set aflame before clicking the camera shutter. Riis realized that this new tool would allow him to shine a light on poverty and that "the darkest corner might be photographed that way."[24]

Armed with his camera and flash, Riis roamed the streets of New York at night, photographing people in sweatshops, cellars, alleys, barrooms, and flophouses. His pictures were not designed as artistic statements but were meant to convey both the humanity of his subjects and the inhumanity of their living conditions. Greenough describes several of the photographs:

> The boy in the photograph *In the Sweat Shop* sits at work surrounded by several idle and threatening men. His bruised eye, apprehensive expression, and busy hands are in sharp contrast to the authoritative and menacing looks and poses of the men. In *Lodgers in a Crowded Bayard Street Tenement: Five Cents a Spot*, Riis showed a room jammed with people and their possessions. Boots, bags, pots, hats, clothes, bedding, and people are stuffed in every corner and hung from the ceiling, and intrude from the edges of the image. They speak more forcefully than any verbal description Riis could have given of the extreme overcrowding in the slums. The floors and ground of Riis' photographs are covered with stains, dirt, water, litter, and garbage; the walls and ceilings are often sagging and covered with peeling paint, plaster, or wallpaper; windows are dark, bare, or broken; tables and chairs are overflowing with tattered possessions.[25]

Riis used his photographs to present slide shows to church and civic reform groups. In 1890, seventeen of the pictures were published in the book *How the Other Half Lives*, one of the earliest books to feature halftone photo reproductions. The book caught the eye of Theodore Roosevelt, then New York City's police commissioner, who used the photographs to push tenement reform, institute building codes, and improve city services to the poor.

Riis was among the first to use the camera to advance a progressive social agenda, but he was not alone. In the early 1900s, Lewis Hine began documenting the conditions of laborers who worked long hours for little pay in miserable, dangerous working conditions. From 1908 to 1918, Hine worked as an investigative photographer for the National Child Labor Committee, a group that crusaded against the widespread practice of using children as young as six to work on farms and in factories, mills, and canneries. Hine traveled more than 50,000 miles (80,467km) across America and took thousands of photographs of children, each one labeled with the child's name, age, type of work performed, and meager amount of pay received. The photographs show small children staring sadly into Hine's lens while shucking oysters, transporting wood, sewing, spinning cotton, operating large machines, and other tasks. The powerful pictures of the exploited children spurred Congress to pass legislation in 1916 outlawing employment of anyone under the age of fourteen.

Photos in Ink

Hine's photographs were taken at a time when technological advances allowed pictures to be disseminated to a widening audience. New printing methods allowed photographs to be printed side-by-side with text in newspapers, books, and magazines, and the invention of the wirephoto let photographers transmit halftone photographs by telephone or telegraph line to distant media outlets. In addition, improvements in cameras meant that photojournalists could take pictures under conditions never before possible. In 1925, Leica introduced the 35mm camera, named for the size of the film it used, which is 1 3/8 inches or 35mm wide. These small cameras could shoot up to forty pictures on a single roll of film, which meant that a photographer could take dozens of pictures of a scene hoping for one good shot. After 1927, the camera could be outfitted with another new invention, the flashbulb, which let photographers take natural-looking photos in low-light conditions.

Margaret Bourke-White snapped the photograph of the Fort Peck dam in Montana that appeared on the first issue of *Life* magazine, November 23, 1936.

The growth of photojournalism was spurred by an increasing number of photographic magazines, such as the *Picture Post* in London, *Paris Match* in France, and the *Daily Graphic* in New York. The large format and superior production of *Life* magazine, founded in 1936, quickly made it the standard by which all other photo magazines were judged. Its pages were filled with high-quality pictures of news events, movie stars, sports heroes, politicians, and scenes from daily life. By the 1940s, the magazine was read by more than half the adults in the United States. Many of the photographers who filled its pages, such as Robert Capa, Alfred Eisenstaedt, and Margaret Bourke-White, became household names and were widely recognized for their remarkable photographic skills. However, many of the photographs were not credited, taken by anonymous photographers who worked for United Press International (UPI) or Associated Press (AP), two of the fifty photographic news services in New York City alone.

Photographing Rural Poverty

In the early 1930s, photojournalism took a new turn when the United States government began hiring photographers to document the effects of the widespread poverty created by the Great Depression. The problem was particularly acute in the countryside, so the Farm Security Administration (FSA) created a special photographic section, called the Historical Unit, to hire photojournalists to document rural poverty. Photographer, curator, historian, and critic John Szarkowski explains why a government bureaucracy was motivated to undertake this effort: "The FSA documentary project was based on the idea that the systematic recording of the visible world provides information that is useful to the understanding and perhaps to the improvement of that world."[26] The photographs taken for the FSA by Dorothea Lange, Walker Evans, Marion Post Wolcott, and Roy Stryker improved the living conditions of the rural poor by spurring public support of government programs to help them. The pictures also proved to be some of the most artistic and critically acclaimed documentary photos of the twentieth century.

Lange, who took nearly four thousand pictures for the FSA, began her career working for ten years as a commercial portrait photographer in San Francisco. In the 1930s, she left commercial work behind and began wandering the streets of the city, documenting unemployment and poverty. Her 1932 photo "White Angel Breadline," showing a depressed, unshaven, hopeless man with an empty tin cup, waiting for food in a breadline, succinctly captured the national mood during the darkest days of the Great Depression.

Dorothea Lange captured one of the most famous images of the Great Depression in her 1936 work "Migrant Mother."

In 1935, Lange went to work for the FSA, and for the next seven years she drove the back roads of America from the Deep South to California and the Pacific Northwest, making portraits of the nation's rural poor. Many of Lange's subjects were homeless families who had lost their farms during the long drought known as the dust bowl and now lived in hobo camps. It was among these struggling Americans that Lange took the famous photo "Migrant Mother," which, according to the Library of Congress, is the picture most requested for publication among the 164,000 that were commissioned by the FSA.

"Migrant Mother" is one of a series of photographs that Lange made of Owens Thompson and her children in February or March of 1936 in Nipomo, California. In 1960, Lange commented:

> I saw and approached the hungry and desperate mother, as if drawn by a magnet. I do not remember how I explained my presence or my camera to her, but I do remember she asked me no questions. I made five exposures, working closer and closer from the same direction. I did not ask her name or her history. She told me her age, that she was thirty-two. She said that they had been living on frozen vegetables from the surrounding fields, and birds that the children killed. She had just sold the tires from her car to buy food. There she sat in that lean-to tent with her children huddled around her, and seemed to know that my pictures might help her, and so she helped me. There was a sort of equality about it.[27]

Margaret Bourke-White

Like Lange, Margaret Bourke-White was a sympathetic photographer who traveled the country photographing dust bowl victims and poor farmers. Bourke-White began her career in the late 1920s creating photo essays of dramatic industrial scenes, such as steel mills and hog-processing facilities, for the business magazine *Fortune*, owned by Henry R. Luce. In 1930, Luce sent

Bourke-White to Germany to photograph the emerging business scene. She managed to get a visa to enter the Soviet Union, which was in the midst of a cultural and industrial revolution. Although the Soviets barred most westerners, officials were so impressed with Bourke-White's portfolio that they gave her complete freedom to take pictures of the nation's people as well as its dams, factories, and farms. The following year, the *New York Times Sunday Magazine* published six articles by Bourke-White, along with her photographs, about the Soviet Union, a place that was a mystery to most Americans.

In 1936, Bourke-White traveled the South with southern author Erskine Caldwell, whose novels depicted the lives of poor white sharecroppers struggling through the Depression. Together, the two collaborated on the 1937 book *You Have Seen Their Faces*, featuring photos of the poorest tenant farmers in the Deep South. Unlike Lange, who photographed her subjects with a quiet dignity, Bourke-White wanted to shock viewers by

As a photographer with the U.S. armed forces during World War II, Margaret Bourke-White captured this image of a Polish concentration camp survivor in May 1945.

presenting unflinching views of destitute and exploited people, riddled with disease and living in decrepit hovels.

Bourke-White's photographic talents prompted Luce to hire her as one of the first photographers for *Life* magazine. The following year, Bourke-White shot "Louisville Flood Victims," a photograph of about a dozen African Americans standing in a

BLURRING THE LINES BETWEEN NEWS AND ART

In recent years, art museums, such as the J. Paul Getty in Los Angeles, have been buying famous news photographs and exhibiting them for the first time as art, as the following Los Angeles Times *article by Christopher Reynolds explains:*

Since 2003, the [J. Paul Getty] museum has bought up several photographic prints that count among the 20th century's most iconic journalistic images of death by violence: [A] Boris Yaro image of the 1968 killing of Robert F. Kennedy; three Eddie Adams pictures of a Vietnamese execution in 1968; and Robert Capa's 1936 image of a Spanish soldier, taken at the moment he suffered a fatal gunshot. . . .

In museums that show photography these days, "there's a willingness to start opening up" and less hand-wringing over what is and isn't art, said Carol McCusker, curator of photography at the Museum of Photographic Arts in San Diego. . . .

Weston Naef, the veteran Getty photography curator who engineered the recent purchases . . . said, the RFK picture . . . "is built from the classic components of works of art, as we've evaluated them from the Renaissance. It's a picture made up of bold patterns of light and dark. You've got the actuality of the dying man, and the emotion of all the people around."

Christopher Reynolds, "Double Exposure of History and Art, in a Shutter's Click," *Los Angeles Times*, January 5, 2007. www.calendarlive.com/galleriesandmuseums/cl-et-artphotos5jan05,0,6406858.story?coll=la-home-headlines.

breadline, waiting to receive assistance after a severe flood drove them from their homes. The startlingly ironic message of the photo comes from a huge billboard behind the flood victims, which shows a family of four white people and a dog, in a car, with the caption "WORLD'S HIGHEST STANDARD OF LIVING. There's no way like the American Way." This photo remains one of the most iconic images from this era of segregation and economic depression.

During World War II, Bourke-White was the only foreign photographer in Russia when Nazi bombs first fell on Moscow and the only female photographer attached to the U.S. armed forces. Bourke-White risked her life as a war correspondent, photographing national leaders, dramatic battlefields, the theater of war, American bombing missions, and overwhelming devastation in Europe. In 1945, she took some of the most shocking pictures of war when she photographed dead and dying Jewish prisoners held in the Nazi concentration camp at Buchenwald after it was liberated by General George Patton's Third Army. Commenting about the experience, Bourke-White stated: "I saw and photographed the piles of naked, lifeless bodies, the human skeletons in furnaces, the living skeletons who would die the next day . . . and tattooed skin [that was made into] lampshades. Using the camera was almost a relief. It interposed a slight barrier between myself and the horror in front of me."[28]

Symbols of Struggle and Victory

Bourke-White's photos were among the first to document the horrors of the Holocaust, but they were only a few frames out of millions that were shot during World War II, which remains among the most photographed wars in history. Depicting events from Asia to western Europe, these photographs provide historians with a wealth of information. Many of these photos were taken by professional photographers who were part of the military forces of Japan, Germany, Italy, and Russia. In the United States, *Life* magazine worked with the armed forces to run a special fifteen-week training program

"VJ Day" by Alfred Eisenstaedt symbolizes the joy that Americans felt on August 15, 1945, the day World War II ended with the United States declaring victory over Japan.

for military photographers and technicians. Renowned British photographer Jorge Lewinski explains why photography was seen as such an important tool:

> Every image, every frame they shot was scrutinized by military experts to assess its usefulness, its suitability in the overall purpose of winning the war. . . . [Censorship] was very strict indeed. Rarely did a picture slip through which the military had not approved. . . . [For] the first and, so far, for the last time, photography was completely harnessed to the war machine itself, an integral part.[29]

Many of the censored photos have been released since the war ended in 1945. Of all the millions taken, several stand out as representative of the war. The official navy photo of the battleships USS *West Virginia* and USS *Tennessee* burning after Japan's attack on Pearl Harbor on December 7, 1941, helped gain instant public support for the United States to declare war on Japan. Later, Robert Capa's photos, taken during a withering barrage of fire as he accompanied American soldiers onto Omaha Beach on D-day, came to symbolize the gritty struggle. And Joe

A DISTURBING POINT OF VIEW

In A New History of Photography, *Fred Ritchin discusses the changing roles of photographers during the Vietnam War as compared to World War II:*

The American government was so eager for publicity that at one point it even paid for some journalists' airplane tickets to Vietnam. With official controls relaxed, journalists were free to roam the land, exploring . . . [and] developing their own deeper interpretations of what was going on. . . . Just as journalists were providing the public with large numbers of photographs, their points of view were diverging from the institutional truths that were being offered by government spokespersons. . . . This divergence changed society's easy relationship with photoreportage. In a general sense, never again could photoreporters be trusted to confirm the point of view of others, because through their photographs they began effectively to challenge the legitimacy of the war that their society . . . [was] sponsoring. Using their supposedly objective cameras they made images that contradicted official thinking . . . a little girl fleeing napalm, a member of the Viet Cong being summarily executed. . . . Rather than authenticating idealized images of Americans—like the photographs taken of heroic soldiers on D-Day or the flag-raising at Iwo Jima—many of the photographs arriving from Vietnam were now . . . providing a disturbing . . . point of view.

Quoted in Michel Frizot, ed., *A New History of Photography.* Köln, Germany: Könemann, 1994, pp. 604–605.

Rosenthal's "Raising of the Flag on Iwo Jima" remains perhaps the most celebrated symbol of victory in that bloody war.

Another photo symbolizing victory was taken by Alfred Eisenstaedt on August 15, 1945, the day the war ended with the United States' declaration of victory over Japan. The picture, "V-J Day," shows a joyous sailor stealing an impromptu kiss from a nurse in the street during a celebration in Times Square in New York City. Speaking of the image, Eisenstaedt said, "The pretty arc of the nurse and the seaman's stylish stance made a 'one in a million' composition. They were very elegant, like sculpture."[30]

Riots and Assassinations

By the 1960s, the sense of unity and purpose in the United States, symbolized by photos in the pages of *Life*, seemed long gone. It was a violent decade marked by war, assassinations, civil rights struggles, and rapid cultural change. During this fiercely polarized era, photography took on a new importance for its ability to reduce complicated issues to a single image and, by doing so, influence public opinion.

In the early part of the decade, as African Americans struggled to gain voting rights and equality amid the harsh racism of the South, Charles Moore, working for the *Montgomery (Alabama) Advertiser*, photographed civil rights leader Martin Luther King Jr. as he was arrested by police. This work led to a contract with *Life*, and Moore went on to photograph dozens of important civil rights marches as well as Ku Klux Klan activities in North Carolina. Moore's photograph "Birmingham Riots, 1963," showing the police spraying black student protesters with fire hoses during a civil rights march, provoked public sympathy for the protesters and helped spur Congress to pass the Civil Rights Act of 1964.

The tumultuous times also provided violent images of public figures who were gunned down by assassins. After President John F. Kennedy was killed on November 22, 1963, *Life* ran a frame-by-frame photo essay, from film footage taken by bystander Abraham Zapruder, of the president being shot in the throat and in the head. The president's assassin, Lee Harvey

Oswald, was murdered two days later, and Robert Jackson's photo "Jack Ruby Shooting Lee Harvey Oswald at a Dallas Police Station" shows Oswald at the instant he was shot.

Several other assassination photos have become icons of those turbulent times. In April 1968, South African documentary photographer Joseph Louw snapped a picture moments after Martin Luther King Jr. was shot in the head on the balcony of the Lorraine Hotel in Memphis. A few months later, photographer Boris Yaro's camera captured the image of Robert Kennedy, President Kennedy's brother, bleeding to death from a gunshot wound to the head after winning the California presidential primary.

Robert Kennedy was shot as he campaigned to end the war in Vietnam. At the time of Kennedy's death, public support for the war was rapidly waning, and many have attributed this change in public opinion to several critical photographs. The first, "Murder of a Vietcong by Saigon Police Chief," was taken

This photo of Birmingham, Alabama, police spraying African American protesters with a fire hose helped turn the tide of public opinion in favor of civil rights legislation in the 1960s.

by AP photographer Eddie Adams on February 1, 1968. The photo shows General Nguyen Ngoc Loan, head of the South Vietnamese national police force, shooting a prisoner, Bay Lop, in the head. Loan's 1998 obituary in the *New York Times* explains the impact of the photograph: "[When] the picture appeared on the front pages of newspapers around the world, the images created an immediate revulsion at a seemingly gratuitous act of savagery that was widely seen as emblematic of a

ROBERT CAPA'S "FALLING SOLDIER"

Robert Capa was a Hungarian-born photographer who was present at some of the bloodiest battles of the twentieth century. Capa gained fame in 1936, covering the Spanish Civil War, when his photo "Loyalist Militiaman at the Moment of Death, Cerro Muriano, September 5, 1936" (also known as "Falling Soldier") appeared on the cover of *Life*. The picture shows a soldier flying backward, arms spread wide, as he is being shot. The caption in *Life* tells the story: "Robert Capa's camera captures a Spanish soldier the instant he is dropped by a bullet through the head in front of Cordoba." The photo gained Capa international recognition nearly overnight.

After the publication of "Falling Soldier," Capa was hired by *Life* to cover World War II. The photographer was part of the amphibious landing on Omaha Beach during the famed Allied D-day invasion of Europe on June 6, 1944. Capa's photographs of that historic day became icons of that war.

Capa liked to say, "If your pictures aren't good enough, you're not close enough," a philosophy that probably contributed to his death. While covering the Korean War in 1954, Capa, trying to get in close for a shot, stepped on a land mine, which killed him instantly. He was forty-one.

Quoted in Maryann Bird, "Robert Capa in Focus," *Time*, June 30, 2002. www.time.com/time/magazine/article/0,9171,901020708-267730,00.html.

seemingly gratuitous war. The photograph . . . was especially vivid, a frozen moment that put a wincing face of horror on the war."[31]

A second photo that had widespread influence in turning public opinion against the war is "Vietnam Napalm," taken by AP photographer Nick Ut in 1972. The grisly image shows a nine-year-old girl running naked down a road, screaming in agony from the jellied gasoline, or napalm, that was dropped on her by U.S. armed forces. Moments after Ut took the picture, he transported the girl to a hospital, and the image, published in newspapers around the world, inspired American doctors to treat the girl, who survived after suffering through dozens of operations. The photographer won a Pulitzer Prize for his picture, which was widely used by antiwar organizations to galvanize support for their movement.

A Lasting Influence

The photographs of Vietnam and earlier wars have achieved the status of art by depicting the emotions and beliefs of millions of people in a single image. Even today, in a world overloaded with imagery from digital cameras, cell phone cameras, twenty-four-hour cable news channels, and billions of Internet pages—a world where photographs peer out from T-shirts, bus benches, billboards, and coffee cups—these great pictures remain icons of their time. But they also continue to influence photojournalists working today. Anyone browsing through a modern newspaper or magazine can see the influence of Capa, Bourke-White, Eisenstaedt, and others. Today, as in times past, photographs depicting violence, love, grief, joy, and countless other emotions continue to mold public opinion.

4

Outsiders and Experimentation

Great artists tend to be social outsiders, a status that allows them to make cutting observations about mass culture in their work. In the late 1950s and throughout the 1960s, a new generation of photographers used their outsider status to challenge the status quo, break the accepted rules of photography, and produce pictures that illuminated a nonconformist vision of a rapidly changing society. These photographers were beatniks, hippies, liberated women, homosexuals, and others who were not embraced by society at large. Their photographs often depicted scenes that were considered shocking and deplorable by the middle-class majority who subscribed to *Life* and *Popular Photography*.

This photographic revolution, like earlier ones, was propelled by changes in technology as well as society. Although the 35mm camera had been in use since the 1920s, the camera was greatly improved in the 1950s when Japanese companies such as Pentax, Canon, and Nikon introduced the single-lens reflex (SLR). Based on the 35mm, the new generation of cameras utilized through-the-lens (TTL) viewing, a system of movable mirrors that allowed the photographer to see the exact image as it would be captured on film. With this system, photographers could focus and set the shutter and exposure times to achieve a perfect picture or create a number of special effects, such as silhouettes and soft focus. The versatility, durability, ease of use, and relatively small size of the SLR made it the choice of millions of photographers by the end of the 1960s, spurring a creative boom that has come to be known as the golden age of photography.

Street Photography

The outsider rebellion in photography began in the 1950s when beatniks, or beats, gathered in big-city coffee houses to read poetry and display their unique works of art. The maverick photographers who traveled in this milieu rejected the objectivity of popular photographers who documented scenes without revealing their personal emotions or political beliefs. Beat photographers rejected objectivity in favor of subjectivity—that is, they injected their undisguised personal beliefs into their photographs. In the late 1950s, Bruce Downes, editor of *Popular Photography*, lamented this development: "Photointellectuals, looking like beatniks . . . [appear] increasingly in such odd places as the rapidly spawning coffee-house picture galleries. . . . [They have] beards, sneakers, and a perverse penchant for poverty." Even worse, wrote Downes, is that they photographed "according to their own standards, and foolishly tried to find a market for their photographs outside the magazines."[32]

Robert Frank, a Swiss immigrant born in 1924, exemplified the type of photographer who irritated Downes. In 1955, Frank bought a run-down jalopy

Improvements made to the 35mm camera in the 1950s made it easier—and more affordable—for the average person to become an amateur photographer.

"EVERYTHING-NESS AND AMERICAN-NESS" OF ROBERT FRANK

When Robert Frank published his book of photos, The Americans, *in 1959, Jack Kerouac, author of the bestseller* On the Road, *wrote the introduction. Kerouac believed that Frank's photos were visual statements similar in tone and content to books and poems of beat authors like himself:*

The humor, the sadness, the EVERYTHING-ness and American-ness of these pictures! Tall thin cowboy rolling butt outside Madison Square Garden New York for rodeo season, sad, spindly, unbelievable—Long shot of night road arrowing forlorn into immensities and flat of impossible-to-believe America in New Mexico under the prisoner's moon—under the whang whang guitar star—Haggard old frowsy dames of Los Angeles leaning peering out the right front window of Old Paw's car on a Sunday gawking and criticizing to explain Amerikay to little children in the spattered back seat—tattooed guy sleeping on grass in park in Cleveland, snoring dead to the world on a Sunday afternoon with too many balloons and sailboats—Old man standing hesitant with oldman cane under old steps long since torn down—Madman resting under American flag canopy in old busted car seat in fantastic Venice California backyard.

Jack Kerouac, introduction to *The Americans,* by Robert Frank. New York: Grossman, 1969, p. ii.

and traveled across America, using his SLR to photograph people in cars, prostitutes on street corners, outlaw bikers, funerals, and ethnic minorities. In 1959, Frank published his pictures in *The Americans*, a book filled with grainy, blurry, poorly exposed photos that broke many traditional rules of photography.

The Americans created an uproar in the media. Downes scathingly wrote that Frank's book presented images "of hate and hopelessness, of desolation and preoccupation with death. . . . It is a world shrouded in an immense gray tragic boredom."[33]

Another critic, William Hogan, wrote in the *San Francisco Chronicle* that the pictures had "no reportorial function."[34] However, those who valued this new way of seeing Americans believed that Frank had captured certain elements of America, infused as it was with loneliness, wide-open spaces, poverty, beauty, and vulgarity interpreted through the lens of the photographer. The introduction to *The Americans*, by beat author Jack Kerouac, described these feelings succinctly: "Robert Frank has captured in these tremendous photographs, taken . . . with the agility, mystery, genius, sadness and strange secrecy of a shadow, . . . scenes that have never been seen before on film. For this he will definitely be hailed as a great artist."[35]

Photographing "Freaks" as Aristocrats

As it turned out, Kerouac was correct, and Frank's photos are now considered classics. Frank went on to direct a series of underground films, but his gritty, subjective photographic style continued to influence photographers throughout the 1960s. One of them was Diane Arbus, who also used her camera to capture the isolation, depression, discomfort, and vulnerability of her subjects.

Arbus was born into an extremely wealthy New York family in 1923. In the 1940s she and her husband, photographer Allan Arbus, worked in the New York fashion industry, taking commercial photos for major advertisers. Dissatisfied with this career, Diane Arbus quit working with her husband in order to take pictures of people who were the complete opposite of the glitzy models she saw every day. With the goal of capturing the faces of society's outcasts, she traveled to nudist camps, mental institutions, roadside carnivals, seedy New York bars, and other places rarely seen by middle-class people. Arbus took time to befriend her potential subjects, be they circus freaks, strippers, bodybuilders, midgets, giants, mentally retarded adults, cross-dressers, eccentrics, or homeless people. Only after establishing trust would Arbus ask her subjects to sit for portraits. Between 1957 and 1970, Arbus created a body of work that is described by photographic scholar Gretchen Garner in *Disappearing Witness:*

> Arbus pictured individuals, although not in the spirit of sympathetic portraits. Her subjects were centered and flash-frozen in the middle of the frame, like specimens in the collection of oddities. Often photographing what she called "freaks," Arbus could manage to make even the most common place, ordinary subjects look freakish.[36]

ARBUS SPEAKS ABOUT FREAKS

Diane Arbus was one of the most influential photographers of the 1960s. In her posthumous collection of writings, An Aperture Monograph, *published in 1972, Arbus describes the nature of photographing nudists, mentally retarded adults, cross-dressers, giants, midgets, and others she refers to as "freaks":*

[I t's] impossible to get out of your skin into somebody else's. And that's what all this is a little bit about. That somebody else's tragedy is not the same as your own. . . . Freaks was a thing I photographed a lot. It was one of the first things I photographed and it had a terrific kind of excitement for me. I just used to adore them. I still do adore some of them. I don't quite mean they're my best friends but they made me feel a mixture of shame and awe. There's a quality of legend about freaks. Like a person in a fairy tale who stops you and demands that you answer a riddle. . . . I do feel I have some slight corner on something about the quality of things. I mean it's very subtle and a little embarrassing to me, but I really believe there are things which nobody would see unless I photographed them.

Diane Arbus, *An Aperture Monograph.* Millerton, NY: 1972. Also available at www.masters-of-photography. com/A/arbus/arbus_articles2.html.

Arbus believed in the nobility of her subjects, however, stating that while most people live in fear of suffering, "Freaks were born with their trauma. They've already passed their test in life. They're aristocrats."[37]

Many critics, however, failed to see the aristocratic in Arbus's work. They saw her merely as a rich girl slumming with outcasts and exploiting their lives. Critics called her work grotesque, hateful, and in bad taste. Renowned best-selling author Norman Mailer offered his opinion in 1963: "Giving a camera to Diane Arbus is like putting a live grenade in the hands of a child."[38]

New Documents

Despite such withering criticism, Arbus's talents were recognized by John Szarkowski, the photography curator at the Museum of Modern Art (MOMA) in New York City. In 1967, when Szarkowski put on an exhibition called New Documents, he showed Arbus's work with that of two other photographers, Garry Winogrand and Lee Friedlander, both of whom were influenced by Frank. This was the first major show for all three photographers, whose work, according to Szarkowski, "showed new developments in documentary photography: disconcerting portraits from Arbus, apparently snapshot like photos from Winogrand, and complex, layered street images from Friedlander."[39]

Like Arbus, Friedlander and Winogrand worked to hold a mirror up to American society. Winogrand was fascinated by body language and the patterns made by limbs, gestures, and postures during spontaneous movements. He noted that "bodies speak in attitudes, in the way they move, walk, sit, lie. They are almost as expressive as when a person opens his mouth and talks."[40]

Unlike Arbus, whose subjects sat for portraits, Winogrand captured people in motion on the streets of New York, sometimes tilting the camera to give the appearance of action to the shot or moving in uncomfortably close to the subject. Photo historian and art director Keith F. Davis describes Winogrand's photos as having "the unpredictability of the street, its restless ebb and flow of human activity . . . a complex mood of energy, longing, and alienation."[41]

Friedlander also worked in the streets, but his photos were less personal and more likely to depict people as insignificant objects lost among the clutter of the city. As Larry Davis and Shereen Davis, founders of the Web site ProFotos.com, write, "The human figures in his street images seem misplaced, surrounded by visual pollution such as signs and advertisements, and disappear under the weight of reflections or under the shadow of the photographer who is taking the picture from outside of the frame."[42]

Of the three photographers whose work was exhibited at the New Documents show, only Friedlander was still working in 2007. Arbus, who suffered from depression, committed suicide in 1971 at the age of forty-seven. In 2004, one of her photographs, "X-mas Tree in a Living Room in Levittown, L.I.," sold for $147,000, while her lesser known prints continue to sell for up to $5,000. Winogrand died from cancer in 1984 at the age of fifty-six. He left behind an amazing body of work—three hundred thousand unedited images and more than two thousand five hundred undeveloped rolls of film.

The Counterculture Experience

The New Documentarians were loners who often worked in a solitary environment. However, the 1960s were a chaotic time when millions of young people in the baby boom generation were taking drugs, experimenting with sex, and trying to change the world with rock and roll. The heart of the cultural transformation was the Haight-Ashbury neighborhood in San Francisco, where nonconformists, called hippies, made themselves the ultimate outsiders by rejecting middle-class values, capitalism, and traditional religion.

Photographer Robert Mark Altman was at the epicenter of the hippie revolution. Having studied photography under Ansel Adams in college, Altman wandered around San Francisco with his camera, documenting the Summer of Love in 1967 before going to work for *Rolling Stone* magazine as its chief photographer in 1969.

Altman's photos of the 1960s and 1970s depict protest marches, love-ins, political revolutionaries like Jerry Rubin, dancing hippies, counterculture theater troupes, and stars such as Dennis Hopper, the Grateful Dead, and the Rolling Stones. With an eye toward composition and a photographer's skill in capturing candid moments, Altman took pictures that are both documentaries of an era and artistic statements in their own right. As Jann Wenner, editor and publisher of *Rolling Stone*, states, "Robert Altman's photography was instrumental in portraying the look and feeling and vitality of the Sixties."[43]

Another *Rolling Stone* photographer, Annie Leibovitz, went to work for the magazine in the early 1970s, and her photos of celebrities were often published on the cover of the magazine. Although her world-famous subjects were hardly outsiders, Leibovitz posed them in unusual settings that wiped away the sheen of celebrity and portrayed them as vulnerable and human. This in itself was revolutionary at the time, as Garner explains: "Leibovitz was shooting in a world already used to the shocking

Annie Leibovitz's work as a *Rolling Stone* photographer launched her reputation as one of today's best photographers. Here, Leibovitz is pictured at the opening of her photo exhibit, "American Music," in 2003.

stratagems of Diane Arbus. [To top them, she] covered Bette Midler with roses, bathed Lauren Hutton in mud, put Woody Allen in a pink-tiled ladies' room . . . backed Patti Smith with a wall of fire, shot John Lennon nude, curled up and attached to [his fully clothed wife] Yoko Ono."[44]

The Father of Color Photography

Leibovitz expertly utilized color in her photos, contrasting, for example, Allen's sallow white skin against the pink background. However, color photography was generally held in contempt in the 1970s by many respected artists who preferred the rich, subtle, and nearly infinite tones of black-and-white film. As Keith Davis writes, to many photographers color "seemed garish and unnatural, suitable only to the worlds of Hollywood, advertising, and the most casual amateur."[45] The general public did not agree, however, and the sale of black-and-white film dropped from 80 million rolls in 1970 to 29 million by 1980.

Among serious art photographers, a few switched to color, creating great controversy. Foremost among them was William Eggleston, born in Tennessee in 1939 and raised on a cotton plantation in the Mississippi Delta. Like most photographers, Eggleston began his career shooting black-and-white. However, in the mid-1970s his one-man show at MOMA featured color photos taken in the Deep South of everyday subjects such as old cars, rusted water tanks, dogs, and an old man holding a pistol. Although the photos had a snapshot quality about them, they were printed using the dye-transfer printing method traditionally used to give advertising photos maximum color saturation. The most striking photograph produced in this manner is the 1973 "Red Ceiling," described by Eggleston:

> When you look at the dye it is like red blood that's wet on the wall. The photograph was [a tricky] exercise for me because I knew that red was the most difficult color to work with. A little red is usually enough, but to work with an entire red surface was a challenge. It was hard

to do. . . . The photograph is still powerful. It shocks you every time.[46]

Although critics called his MOMA show boring and banal, Eggleston soon became known, half humorously, as the "father of color photography."[47] While obviously not true (Eisenstaedt had been using color since the late 1940s), Eggleston was the founder of what would come to be called New Color photography. Through the rest of the 1970s and into the 1980s, photographers such as Joel Meyerowitz, Jan Groover, and Mitch Epstein showed how color tones in film, when exposed by an expert photographer, could be as emotional, jarring, or soothingly beautiful as black-and-white.

"An Unforgiving Light"

By the mid-1980s, color photography was well accepted by professionals, galleries, and photo magazines. And the groundwork laid by the New Colorists continued to resonate throughout the art world. In Great Britain, Martin Parr was first inspired to work in saturated colors after viewing the work of Eggleston and

British photographer Martin Parr stands next to one of his controversial photos from the series The Last Resort during a 2004 exhibit.

Meyerowitz. Parr, however, had a keen eye for social commentary and found a way to combine garish colors in lurid photos that provide a critical look at modern society, consumerism, and the relationships between people and food. Parr's breakthrough series, The Last Resort, shot at the run-down seaside resort of New Brighton, England, is described on Eyestorm, an online art and photography gallery:

> It showed New Brighton and its holidaymakers in an unforgiving light: guzzling Coke and Pepsi, hot-dogs and crisps; burned horrible shades of pink and heavily overweight; naked babies and young children playing next to overflowing rubbish bins and paddling off concrete piers in eddies of sodden trash. There was no safe veil of nostalgia, nothing subdued by black and white.[48]

The controversial photos helped cement Parr's status as a brash new voice in British photography. When the Last Resort photos were published in a book in 1986, Parr's critics labeled him cruel and exploitive, while his supporters hailed his use of

wit, satire, and brutal honesty. Parr continued to produce photographs critical of consumerist attitudes with the 1989 series The Cost of Living. In the 1990s, he traveled to Germany and Japan to document what Eyestorm calls "mass tourism, mass consumption, mass marketing, global homogenization. . . . Parr was observing the First World: the overstimulated and the overfed."[49]

Perfect or Pandering?

Some critics considered Parr's photos offensive, but by this time many outsider artists were using the outrageous to express their attitudes, opinions, and biting criticism. In so doing, a few leveraged photographic controversy into worldwide fame. One of the most notorious artists of any type in the 1980s, Robert Mapplethorpe, was initially known for his beautiful black-and-white portraits of celebrities such as actress Isabella Rossellini and rock singers Iggy Pop and Patti Smith. However, Mapplethorpe, who was a homosexual, became a lightning rod for controversy when he used a $15,000 grant from the National Endowment for the Arts (NEA) to partially fund a full retrospective of his work, called The Perfect Moment, at the Whitney Museum in New York. Among the dozens of photographs in the exhibit, a few showed sexually explicit images of gay men. The content of the erotic photos came to the attention of North Carolina's Republican senator Jesse Helms, who began a crusade against public funding of controversial art which continues to this day.

In 1990, The Perfect Moment was due to appear at the Corcoran Gallery of Art in Washington, D.C., but the exhibition was canceled at the last minute because the gallery feared that Helms would cut its funding. The show was instead moved to the Center for Contemporary Art in Cincinnati. The curator, Dennis Barrie, was arrested for "pandering obscenity," although the controversial pictures were displayed behind a curtain and could be viewed only by adults. At Barrie's trial, a judge declared Mapplethorpe's work to be of artistic value, and the charges against the curator were dropped. However, by that time, partially because of Mapplethorpe's work, the Senate had rewritten the rules for the NEA, drastically cutting the organization's funding and barring grants to individual artists. Mapplethorpe himself was not able to testify at the obscenity trial. The photographer died from AIDS on March 9, 1989, at the age of forty-two.

Phototherapy

Even as Mapplethorpe was depicting men in ways not often seen by the public, female photographers were using their art to redefine the roles of women. One such photographer, Jo Spence, born in England in 1934, was a feminist who used her camera in the 1970s to document women's roles in the workplace. By the end of the decade, Spence labeled her work "counter-photography." This is a style meant to examine the true relationships between family members as opposed to the cheerful way they are portrayed in traditional family photographs. As Spence explained, "Within all households, forms of domestic warfare are continually in progress, and although we live this daily power struggle, it is censored . . . [and] transformed into icons of . . . harmony within family photography."[50]

While Spence's view of "domestic warfare" was upsetting to some, she continued "working against the grain of existing mythologies"[51] after she was diagnosed with breast cancer in 1982. Rather than keep her medical condition secret and private, Spence decided to use her cancer as a photographic opportunity. In doing so, she developed what she called phototherapy to document and thus take control of traumatic events such as mammograms, attempts at alternative healing, and the aftereffects of surgery. Commenting on phototherapy, Spence stated, "Passing through the hands of the medical orthodoxy can be terrifying when you have breast cancer. I [was] determined to document for myself what was happening to me. Not to be merely the object of their medical discourse but to be the active subject of my own investigation."[52]

Spence's pictures were exhibited in the show Picture of Health? in 1986, six years before the photographer died of cancer. Today her photos and articles on breast cancer and phototherapy, published on the Internet, are still of interest to those who suffer from the disease.

"The Diary I Let People Read"

New York native Nan Goldin used her camera to document disorders of a different type—those caused by AIDS, heroin addiction, and domestic abuse. Goldin embraced photography, which she described as "the diary I let people read,"[53] as a healing art after a traumatic childhood marred by her sister's suicide and her own life in a series of foster homes.

Goldin came of age during the punk rock era, and her snapshot-style photographs depict transvestites, drug users, bisexuals, and homosexuals in New York's Bowery, a neighborhood at the center of the punk movement. Moving beyond the style perfected by Arbus, Goldin worked with color slide film, and the resulting prints are glossy and colorful, much like the nightlife and the characters who fill the frames.

In the early 1980s, Goldin assembled photos of drunken parties, drag queens, and even evidence of beatings by her boyfriend into a slide show. This forty-five-minute-long exhibit, called Ballad of Sexual Dependency, was shown at punk rock clubs in New York, accompanied by loud rock music. In 1986, Goldin took the exhibit to Europe, giving her slide show at the Edinburgh and Berlin film festivals. In the years that followed, she continued to document the lives of her friends, many of whom were dying of AIDS. Primary among them was actress Cookie Mueller, whom the photographer had known since 1976. After Mueller died of AIDS in 1989, Goldin put together

Nan Goldin, under a projection of one of her images, used her photography to document the lives of her friends and their experiences with AIDS, addiction, domestic abuse, and other issues.

Nan one month after being battered, 1984

Awardee

GARRY WINOGRAND'S "UNUSUAL PEOPLE"

The following description of Garry Winogrand's photographic style by Larry Davis and Shereen Davis appeared on the ProFotos.com Web site:

Winogrand's subject was America. He documented the city and the urban landscape, concentrating on its unusual people and capturing odd juxtapositions of animate and inanimate objects. . . . Winogrand made the city, the zoo, the airport, and the rodeo his home, and spent endless hours photographing there. A photographer of this sort is a wanderer, constantly roaming the globe, clicking the shutter wherever he went.

Winogrand's photographs catch that odd moment where unrelated activities coincided, and it is the nature of these juxtapositions that sets his work apart from other photographers. He photographed all subjects with the same detached but observant eye, making complex compositions through which the viewer weaves. In his first book *The Animals* (1969), photographs of people and animals at the zoo are both a humorous and sarcastic look at the human race. The animals exhibit human-like qualities and when photographed in relation to humans it is often hard to tell who is performing for whom. In one shot an elderly woman wearing diamond studded pointy sunglasses looks out from the lower right hand corner of the image. Behind her two rhinos butt heads, their bodies echoing the shape of her glasses. . . . Much of the action on Winogrand's photographs is implied. The pictures exist before, in anticipation of that which is about to occur.

Larry Davis and Shereen Davis, "Garry Winogrand," ProFotos.com, 2006. www.profotos.com/education/referencedesk/masters/masters/garrywinogrand/garrywinogrand.shtml.

the Cookie Portfolio, a show in her friend's honor. The fifteen photographs of this exhibition documented Goldin's relationship with Mueller from the early parties they attended until Mueller's funeral thirteen years later. These photos were exhibited in many shows both in the United States and internationally.

In addition to Mueller, Goldin photographed—and cared for—many friends with AIDS. Throughout the years of sadness and loss, Goldin credited photography for helping her survive. As she stated in a 2003 interview, "photography saved my life. Every time I go through something scary, traumatic, I survive by taking pictures."[54]

Documents of Changing Times

Nonconformists like Goldin and Arbus put their mark on the photographic arts with personal statements about death, disorders, and diseases. Like Altman's, their work was strongly influenced by a burgeoning underground culture. What the photographers have in common is the outsider's viewpoint and the desire to travel in circles far removed from the safe, conventional world of the middle classes.

Perhaps it is not surprising that *Life* magazine ceased publication in 1972. By that time the world would have been unrecognizable to someone living in the 1950s during the magazine's heyday. The photos taken by the outsiders document how those times changed, how the world was transformed by the views and values of hippies, homosexuals, punk rockers, and other outsiders in the 1960s, 1970s, and 1980s.

5

Pixels and Pictures

The art of photography did not exist until inventors discovered a chemical process for recording images in the late 1830s. For the next century and a half, chemistry and photography were inextricably linked. By manipulating the way light particles interact with silver halide crystals and developing agents, photographers changed the way people see the world. All that began to change in 1987 when scientists working for Kodak created the world's first megapixel charge-coupled device (CCD) sensor. This integrated circuit was capable of recording 1.4 million pixels, or picture elements, and converting them into information that could be read by a computer. While other more primitive CCD sensors had been used by scientists, the military, and NASA since the 1970s, this new sensor was the first one capable of producing a decent-quality 5 x 7 inch (13 x 18 cm) photograph. With this new invention the digital photography age was born.

In 1991, Kodak sold the first digital camera, the DCS-100, mounted in a Nikon body and attached to a huge side pack that held a 200 MB hard drive capable of holding 156 images. The DCS-100 sold for $13,000 and had a resolution of 1.3 megapixels. By way of comparison, a camera sold today with similar resolution fits into the palm of the hand and can be purchased for about $20.

Around the same time that the DCS-100 was put into production, Adobe launched Photoshop 1.0, the first computer software program made to manipulate digital images. In the years that followed, continued development of digital technology changed nearly every aspect of life, including photography. Digital cameras improved in quality, photo printers were developed, software improved, prices fell, and in 2000 the first digital cameras began to appear in cell phones. By 2007, more than three-quarters of all cameras sold were digital, and in the world of commercial photography, 70 percent of all professionally taken photographs were digital images.

The digital camera has heralded a photography revolution. Using it in conjunction with computers, scanners, and advanced drawing, painting, photographic, and three-dimensional modeling software programs, photographers can create photomontages, photo-collages, and enhanced photographs. And these images can be easily displayed on Web pages, Internet galleries, and other computerized formats.

With the introduction of digital cameras in the 1990s, chemicals and film gave way to pixels and microchips.

"Endless Possibilities for Manipulation"

Every new photographic innovation provides photographers with new methods for creating pictures, methods that are often questioned by critics and the viewing public. Digital photography—photographs manipulated with computers and software—has generated debate and, on occasion, controversy.

One issue concerns the artistic value of imperfect film when compared to crystal-clear digital images. The new cameras have eliminated roll film, which could be ruined or compromised before or during processing. However, darkroom errors created some of the most memorable images of the twentieth century. For example, after Robert Capa risked his life to shoot four rolls of film during the D-day invasion of World War II, a darkroom technician, in a hurry to print the pictures, turned the film drier up too high. This mistake melted all but eleven frames. However, the surviving pictures, while damaged, had a gritty, blurred quality that portrayed the emotional events of the day in a uniquely artistic way. A similar photo, taken with a digital camera and manipulated after the fact with Photoshop, would not have had the same honesty and integrity as Capa's brutally realistic images.

In 2000, digital cameras were introduced to cell phones.

A second issue concerns the manipulation of digital photos. In 2006, the Reuters news service widely disseminated a picture of Beirut, Lebanon, burning after an Israeli bombing

attack. The picture was taken by freelance photojournalist Adnan Hajj, who had sold numerous photos to Reuters over ten years. However, Hajj used software to add black plumes of smoke rising over the city where, in reality, there was only a small amount of gray smoke from the attack. While Hajj's manipulation made for a more dramatic photo, it created an uproar. Critics charged the photographer with exaggerating the severity of the attack, not to create a more artistic photo, but to make a political point against the Israelis. Hoy explains how such problems have changed the nature of the photographic arts:

> [Digital] photography, with its endless possibilities for manipulation, has blurred the lines between photographic "reality" and artistic invention. Since the early days of photography, images have been constructed through the creative use of composition, camera angle, lighting, and shutter speed. But when the image is made, that particular moment of reality, however creatively produced, has by and large been captured. With digital photos, on the other hand, tripping the shutter is just the beginning. Even for the amateur photographer, computer manipulations can do anything from removing red-eye . . . to plopping a penguin on the shoulder of Aunt Millie. . . . And therein lies the contradiction of the digital revolution. Digital cameras can be used as a straightforward system of photography or they can be used to create something quite different from the photographic traditions of the past century and a half—artificially generated images that bear little

Digital photography eliminates the need for darkrooms and enlargers to process photographic film.

Many feel that digital photos stored on CDs and DVDs lack the appeal of flipping through an old family photo album.

relationship to "reality" and share more characteristics with painting than with conventional photography.[55]

A third issue concerns the quality and permanence of digital pictures. Today, daguerreotypes, platinum prints, and incredibly vivid black-and-white photos taken over a century ago are still displayed in galleries and museums. These prints were laboriously produced with expensive archival materials by photographers who created them to last for generations. While digital photos may be stored on semipermanent formats such as CDs and DVDs, these discs will someday become obsolete, as will the computers that read them. And most of the prints made on photo printers lack the quality and permanence of old-style film prints. While antique stores today are filled with old stereoscopic prints and ancient family photos, few experts imagine that the digital photo prints of the twenty-first century will be available to curious viewers a hundred years hence.

Seeing the World in New Ways

Whatever the difference between film and digital photographs, there is little doubt that the world has embraced the new medium. Digital techniques are used without apology by artists who, in Hoy's words, want their photos to "share more characteristics with painting." These photographers, instead of manipulating microscopic silver crystals, can artfully create a picture by rearranging the pixels that make up a digital image. Describing this process, photographer John Lund says, "I always wanted to be a painter, and I also love photography. . . . So now I'm happy because I get to paint with images. Anything I can think up, I can create in a photographic reality. To me, that's the ultimate joy of being a photographer."[56]

ADVANTAGES OF DIGITAL PHOTOGRAPHY

In The Book of Photography Anne H. Hoy describes some advantages of digital cameras compared to film cameras:

If ever a photographic innovation played to the human desire for instant gratification, it would have to be the digital camera. . . . [With] today's digital cameras, photographers can see the result of their efforts virtually instantaneously. . . . The reasons for the massive switch to digital are simple: convenience and control. Digital camera users don't have to purchase or carry bulky rolls of film—one reusable memory card can hold hundreds of images. LCD panels on digital cameras enable users to preview and delete bad shots. Once the images are downloaded into a computer, they can be enhanced, cropped, and transmitted electronically over the Internet, and high-quality prints can be made at home on a digital printer. For the average photographer, digital has become easier to use—and in many ways more fun to shoot—than film.

Anne H. Hoy, *The Book of Photography*. Washington, DC: National Geographic, 2005, p. 400.

Todd Walker was one of the first photographers to use pixels to blur the lines between photography and painting. He began his career after World War II as a freelance commercial photographer, but by the 1970s he was known for his artistic experiments with dyes, blueprints, gum dichromate, photo silkscreens, and other techniques that produced unconventional, colorful, distorted imagery. In the 1980s, Walker wrote his own computer program so he could continue to produce unmatched abstract images. His 1983 photograph "Opuntia, Digitized," of a prickly pear cactus (opuntia), is one of the first digital photographic images produced by a successful fine art photographer.

As digital imagery has flourished since that time, the subjectivism seen in the 1960s, 1970s, and 1980s has been replaced by what some call a new or neo-pictorialism. This movement is based on the pictorialism of the late nineteenth century, when photographers smeared their lenses with petroleum jelly and raked their prints with needles to give their work a painterly appearance. With the new pictorialism, photographers can use software programs such as Corel's Painter to achieve an infinite variety of artistic effects. But unlike the old pictorialism, digital photography allows the photographer to mix and match artistic styles such as hyperrealism, pictorialism, and surrealism within a single picture, a technique that is considered impossible with "straight" photography. Judged by the standard of any great art, such compositions should present a photographer's vision while stirring an emotional response in the viewer. Commenting on the possibilities of the digital medium, Mexican photographer Pedro Meyer, one of the pioneers of contemporary photography, states, "I would hope that we are at a stage when we can actually liberate photography and unleash its great creative potential in order to make great documentary fictions that make us see the world in new ways."[57]

Photomontage

Much of the digital art photography seen today consists of separate images that have been combined to produce a single picture. This technique, called photomontage, has its roots in the

Artist Robert Silvers stands with his photomontage of actor Jim Carrey. Silvers created software that assembles tiny images into a larger image.

1850s when artificial environments were created by photographers like Oscar Rejlander and Henry Peach Robinson. While the nineteenth-century photographers laboriously pieced together negatives and prints in a darkroom, modern photomontage artists can create a nearly infinite variety of images with cameras, computers, and software programs such as Photoshop, Pixel Image Editor, and the freeware program

A Career as a Freelance Photographer

The photographs of Ansel Adams, Diane Arbus, and other professionals have inspired countless people to pursue a career as freelance photographers. Like musicians, writers, and other artists, only the most talented and driven photographers attain international success. There are millions, however, who work as self-employed photographers in a variety of fields, including advertising, travel, Web development, journalism, criminal investigation, portraiture, fine art, and scientific fields such as medical photography. Freelance photographers may also license the use of their photographs through stock-photo agencies that sell the right to use photographs to magazines and other customers. These agencies require a sizable portfolio of commercially appealing pictures.

Photographers face a wide variety of working conditions. Those employed by advertising agencies may work a forty-hour week; those who make their living as photojournalists may work long, irregular hours, often in uncomfortable or dangerous surroundings when covering accidents, natural disasters, civil unrest, or military conflicts.

Most photographers spend only a small portion of their work schedule actually taking pictures. They do spend considerable time editing images on a computer—if they use a digital camera—and looking for new business.

GIMP, which stands for GNU Manipulation Program. The goal of the digital montagists is to create a single picture that combines photography, painting, graphics, and illustration.

British photographer John Goto combines the above elements with theatrics in order to make political statements. For example, Goto's series Floodscape brings together images depicting Europe after global warming has created massive flooding in formerly populated areas. Although the topic is serious, the images often make points with humor. For example, in the photo "Embarkation from Ham," a boat carrying well-dressed partiers, self-absorbed and oblivious to the rising waters, floats down the Thames River past flooded buildings and statues. Meanwhile, the causes of global warming, jets and boats, continue to pollute the air. According to Goto's narrative of the photomontage,

> [A] group of young revelers set off on the Thames, despite the rising waters. . . . The punt [narrow open boat] they travel in is driven by a powerful, but smoky, outboard motor. The partygoers drink champagne and play with their digital toys amidst designer carrier bags containing acquisitions purchased on their shopping expedition. . . . The darkening sky is crowded with passenger jets flying to and from nearby Heathrow airport.[58]

The series follows the revelers through eight photomontages as their little boat is superimposed in front of submerged London landmarks such as the Millennium Dome and Canary Wharf.

In a more recent series, New World Circus, Goto uses his photomontage technique to express his feelings about the Iraq War. Composed as a series of circus scenes, each of the photomontages combines parody, satire, and humor. The photos show acrobats, jugglers, clowns, a ringmaster, an illusionist, a magician, and other typical circus characters parodying various aspects of the war and occupation, such as Iraqis pulling down a statue of Saddam Hussein after the initial invasion. To create the twenty-two photomontages in the series, Goto rented a studio and costumes and photographed models, mannequins, and friends and neighbors playing the parts of circus characters. Goto worked twelve hours a day in front of his computer to paste together the photographs, which have been displayed in galleries and on the Internet with a musical soundtrack.

Photography, Art, and Cinema

Goto's photographs have a cinematic quality that has long been part of the digital photography art movement. Canadian photographer Jeff Wall also creates montages in a genre he describes as "cinematographic," or in the style of a movie. Unlike Goto, however, Wall seamlessly blends photographs into a picture that looks as if it is a single snapshot. Only upon further inspection does the viewer notice that the photos contain bizarre or complex elements that could not possibly be real.

To create a photograph, Wall digitally combines up to one hundred images that were shot in a studio or on location at different times, sometimes over the course of several years. With the aid of a computer, Wall flawlessly blends the still lifes, action shots, and isolated figures into photos called mise-en-scènes, a term used to describe the actors, scenery, and properties on a stage or movie set. Commenting on the complex, time-consuming process, Wall states, "When I began working on the computer I realized you don't have to do it all at once. Of course it's exciting trying to get everything in one shot, but working digitally slowed things down. It made the process more complicated and, I hope, deeper."[59]

Wall's photos are reproduced as large transparencies, some more than 6 by 8 feet (1.8 by 2.4 m). These are mounted in light boxes where they are backlit. This arrangement gives the photographs a theatrical element as if they were projected onto a movie screen. By virtue of their size, Wall's mise-en-scènes are tailored to be hung on gallery walls in the manner of large paintings.

Wall uses his photographs to comment on social problems such as racism, sexism, and other issues often based on themes in paintings or classic books. One of the photographer's most renowned pictures, "After the Invisible Man," was inspired by the 1952 Ralph Ellison novel *Invisible Man*. The opening scene of Ellison's book describes an African American man who falls into an abandoned cellar during a New York riot. He decides to live there, hiding forever from the injustices and racism of society. While describing the man's underground apartment, Ellison mentions that it is lit by 1,369 lightbulbs illegally connected to a power box. Wall's photograph of the scene, a composite of dozens of photographs that took three years to shoot and assemble, is described by Jed Perl in the *New Republic:*

> Working in his Vancouver studio, Wall re-created Ellison's basement setting; he shows us every bit of junk that the invisible man has corralled in his subterranean hideaway. Even as all the thrift-shop clutter in Wall's huge photograph threatens to deaden the story's symbolic power, the light bulbs strung up on the ceiling like demented Christmas decorations pull the composition together and lend it a crazy magic. . . . Wall brings such a concentrated, obsessive attention to every detail that the photograph achieves, overall, its own kind of heightened, almost spooky verisimilitude [appearance of reality]. The color is remarkable. A peculiar, subdued yet ebullient brown-gray luminosity suffuses the image. And there, amid all the jumbled stuff in the shabby basement, is Ellison's protagonist, who sits in his undershirt, listening to a record. . . . There is a winning reticence to Wall's portrait of Ellison's hero, whom we see from the side, with only a tantalizing glimpse of his gentle, pensive face.[60]

Combining Classical Elements

Wall uses computers to create realistic photographs from disparate elements. Other digital photographers use camera and computer to create dreamlike photos with little basis in reality. For example, Marisol Fernández creates photomontages that are made up of dozens of separate elements combined to produce humorous, poignant, or striking photographs. Fernández's pictures are digitized versions of the world based on themes seen in classical paintings. Her work appears on the ZoneZero photo gallery, a Web site that hosts the work of more than a thousand photographers from all over the world.

Philippe Abril is more than inspired by classical paintings—he sometimes incorporates them directly into his composite photos. For example, Abril's "Le Cri" uses Edvard Munch's famous painting *The Scream* as a backdrop for a photo of Abril striking a similar pose, clutching his head with his mouth agape, like the character in the painting. In other pictures, Abril digitizes old photographic portraits from the nineteenth and twentieth centuries and uses them for subject matter, pasting them into paintings by artists such as Renaissance painter Lucas Cranach or modern American painter Jean-Michel Basquiat. The results are provocative and disjointed, with anonymous people from old family albums residing in paintings most often seen in art museums.

JOHN GOTO DESCRIBES DIGITAL PHOTOGRAPHY

John Goto, known for photomontages that make satirical and poignant comments about society, discusses digital photography and photo manipulation on his New World Circus Web site:

Photography has changed irreversibly with the advent of digitalization. During the pre-history of photography much effort and ingenuity was expended on the problem of fixing the image. Digital processes have undone all this, destabilizing the image again and making it fluid and mutable. Elements can readily be extracted or sampled and edited into new composites; they can be grafted together with other media and new hybrids formed; they can be transmitted rapidly across a variety of informational systems at low cost and accessed, stored or remade by viewers worldwide. All certainty regarding the authenticity of the subject is now lost. Digital photography's amorphous quality resembles that of the dream, the metaphor, the hallucination, the joke, the vision and all manner of trickery, pranks, [sleights] of hand and illusions. Digital photography reclaims the freedoms once enjoyed by narrative painting, and indeed shares many of the same methods.

John Goto, "Disunited States," New World Circus, 2004. http://johngoto.org.uk/NewWorldCircus/dis united_states.html.

Abril mainly works with Adobe Photoshop to create his pictures, but Dutch artist Kees Roobol uses a wide variety of sophisticated software that has been created only in the past decade. This enables him to create photographs with stunning three-dimensional figures arranged in virtual scenes reminiscent of science fiction and fantasy stories.

Roobol is inspired by the painting genre known as magic realism, developed since the 1920s, in which fantastical elements appear in an otherwise realistic setting. This style incorporates rich sensory details and elements of legend or folklore portrayed against a mundane background. Roobol creates magic realism by photographing friends, actors, and models in front of ancient churches and castles or in historical reconstructions like those found in history museums. Using Bryce 3-D Imagine software along with Painter, Photoshop, Raydream, and Poser programs, Roobol spends from one hundred to two hundred hours piecing together a single photo. Although he can produce only five or six images a year in this fashion, the results are unique. Photos such as "The Gathering of Fates" combine dramatic, cloudy skies, brilliantly colored flowers, and figures wearing traditional Dutch costumes.

Photo-Collage

Photographers such as Roobol and Goto often begin a picture by creating a backdrop and then layering different photographs into the scene to create a photomontage. Those who work with a different technique, called photo-collage, cut out pieces of a picture and paste them into a new image. When layered together with several photographs, the finished photo-collage may be unlike anything in the real world.

The first photo-collagists were the surrealists of the 1920s like Man Ray and Hanna Höch. The photos they produced were instantly recognizable as collages because of their layered, irregularly lined surfaces. In the digital age, however, photo-collages are not created with scissors and glue but may be effortlessly blended. As J.D. Jarvis, curator of the Museum of Computer Art (MOCA), writes:

[The] capabilities of digital tools have expanded this genre far from anything ever before possible. To the simple processes of "cut and paste" have been added instant resizing, reversing the image, color toning, texturizing, advanced compositing and layering techniques and a whole host of digital effects. The whole genre of collage has been energized by the vision of people who might never have considered themselves artists or by established artists who have found digital collage techniques can now bring a wider range of materials and image sources into one composition.[61]

The MOCA Web site displays the photo-collage work of several artists, including Damnengine (real name Dennis Sibeijn), a Dutch audio-visual designer who pastes together artwork, photographs, and scanned objects. His collages contain otherworldly, often disturbingly monstrous figures that would be at home in a painting by surrealist Salvador Dali.

Another photo-collagist whose photos are displayed on MOCA works in a similar manner. Turkish graphic design artist Gulner Guvenc created her Chtulhu People series using a scanner to record images of seashells that she combined with photographs of a friend. According to Jarvis, the results show a race of "mythical sea people with exoskeletons resembling seashells and decidedly humanoid features."[62]

Great Photographers

Photographers like Guvenc and Damnengine are creating photographic images unlike any ever seen before. In doing so, they have joined the ranks of photographers who have been blazing new paths in photography since 1839. However, while digital tools open new doors for photographers to enter, it still takes creative vision and an artistic eye to make a picture that is considered fine art. As photographer and artist Larry Bolch writes, "Photography is not an art. It is a medium through which artists may create art."[63]

Notes

Introduction: A Rich History

1. Quoted in Digicam Help, "Light and Digital Photography," 2007. www.digicamhelp.com/learn/working-with-light.
2. Quoted in Kodak, "A History of Kodak: 1878–1929," 2006. www.kodak.com/US/en/corp/kodakHistory/1878_1929.shtml.

Chapter 1: A New Way to See the World

3. Quoted in Floyd Rinhart and Marion Rinhart, *The American Daguerreotype*. Athens, GA: University of Athens Press, 1981, p. 40.
4. Quoted in Michel Frizot, ed., *A New History of Photography*. Köln, Germany: Könemann, 1994, p. 42.
5. Peter Marshall, "Photography in the 1840s," About Photography, 2007. http://photography.about.com/library/weekly/aa061702b.htm.
6. Quoted in William L. Camp, "Painting With the Sun: Early Photographers of Montrose, PA, 1842—1886," Local History, 2003. http://home.stny.rr.com/wlcamp/Montrose.htm.
7. Rinhart and Rinhart, *The American Daguerreotype*, p. 55.
8. Quoted in Frizot, *A New History of Photography*, p. 158.

Chapter 2: A Fine Art Movement

9. Anne H. Hoy, *The Book of Photography*. Washington, DC: National Geographic, 2005, p. 237.
10. Robert Leggat, "A History of Photography," Robert Leggat's Homepage, July 24, 2006. www.rleggat.com/photohistory/history/robinson.htm.
11. Quoted in Leggat, "A History of Photography."
12. Sarah Greenough, Joel Snyder, David Travis, and Colin Westerbeck, *On the Art of Fixing a Shadow*. Boston: Bulfinch, 1989, pp. 129–30.
13. Quoted in Jon Stringer, "The Life and Work of Dr. P.H. Emerson," Net Communications, 2006. http://people.netcom.co.uk/j.stringe/page3.html.
14. Quoted in Frizot, *A New History of Photography*, p. 311.
15. Quoted in Anthony Troncal, "Yesterday, Today and Tomorrow: The Camera Club of New York, 1888–2002," Camera Club of New York, 2002. www.cameraclubofnewyork.org/history_long.html.
16. Quoted in Frizot, *A New History of Photography*, p. 314.
17. John Stevenson, "Platinum Photography," Collector's Guide, 2007. www.collectorsguide.com/fa/fa031.shtml.

18. Quoted in Mark Katzman, "Straight Photography," Art of Photogravure, 2007. www.photogravure.com/history/chapter_straightphotography.html.

19. Andy Grundberg, "Photography View: What Was Cubism's Impact," *New York Times*, December 13, 1981. http://query.nytimes.com/gst/full page.html?res=9D00EED61438F93 0A25751C1A967948260.

20. Metropolitan Museum of Art, Department of Photographs, "Photography and Surrealism," 2006. www.metmuseum.org/toah/hd/phsr/hd_phsr.htm.

21. Quoted in Hoy, *The Book of Photography*, p. 288.

22. Greenough et al., *On the Art of Fixing a Shadow*, p. 231.

23. Quoted in Donald Krehbiel, "f/64 Manifesto," Minox, Metol & Macintosh, 2006. www.kcbx.net/~mhd/1intro/f64.htm.

Chapter 3: Capturing the Human Drama

24. Quoted in Louise Ware, *Jacob A. Riis: Police Reporter, Reformer, Useful Citizen*. New York: Appleton-Century, 1938, p. 25.

25. Greenough et al., *On the Art of Fixing a Shadow*, pp. 137–38.

26. John Szarkowski, *Photography Until Now*. Boston: Bulfinch, 1989, pp. 213, 215.

27. Quoted in Library of Congress, "Dorothea Lange's 'Migrant Mother' Photographs in the Farm Security Administration Collection: An Overview," December 15, 2005. www.loc.gov/rr/print/list/128_migm.html.

28. Quoted in University of Iowa, "Margaret Bourke-White Photos for *Life* Magazine at Buchenwald, 1945," 2005. www.uiowa.edu/poli cult/politicalphotos/holocaust2.html.

29. Jorge Lewinski, *The Camera at War*. New York: Simon & Schuster, 1980, p. 95.

30. Alfred Eisenstaedt, "V-J Day Kiss, Part 1," *Life*, 1995. www.life.com /Life/special/kiss01a.html.

31. Quoted in Wellesley College, "VCEXEC," 2007. www.wellesley.edu /Polisci/wj/Vietimages/vcexec.htm.

Chapter 4: Outsiders and Experimentation

32. Quoted in Joel Eisinger, *Trace and Transformation*. Albuquerque: University of New Mexico Press, 1995, p. 130.

33. Quoted in Eisinger, *Trace and Transformation*, p. 130.

34. Quoted in Eisinger, *Trace and Transformation*, p. 130.

35. Jack Kerouac, introduction to *The Americans*, by Robert Frank. New York: Grossman, 1969, p. i.

36. Gretchen Garner, *Disappearing Witness*. Baltimore: Johns Hopkins University Press, 2003, p. 130.

37. Quoted in Diane Arbus: An Unofficial Website, 2004. www.dianearbus.net/infocus.htm.

38. Quoted in A Gallery for Fine Photography, "Diane Arbus," 2001. www.agallery.com/Pages/photographers/arbus.html.

39. Quoted in Larry Davis and Shereen Davis, "Lee Friedlander," ProFotos.com, 2006. www.profotos.com/education/referencedesk/masters/masters/le efriedlander/leefriedlander.shtml.

40. Quoted in Keith F. Davis, *An American Century of Photography*.

Kansas City, MO: Hallmark Cards, 1999, p. 306.

41. Davis, *An American Century of Photography*, p. 306.

42. Davis and Davis, "Lee Friedlander."

43. Quoted in Robert Altman, "Curriculum Vitae," 2006. www.altman photo.com/curriculum_vitae.html.

44. Garner, *Disappearing Witness*, pp. 181–82.

45. Davis, *An American Century of Photography*, p. 303.

46. Quoted in Photo.net, "William Eggleston DVD," 2006. http://photo.net.

47. William Eggleston, "Artist Bio," 2005. www.egglestontrust.com.

48. Eyestorm, "Martin Parr," 2003. www.eyestorm.com/feature/ED2n_article.asp?article_id=237&artist_id=12.

49. Eyestorm, "Martin Parr."

50. Quoted in David Evans, "A Primer," Belfast Exposed, 2005. www.belfast exposed.org/themedpackages/index.php?id=2&sid=35.

51. Jo Spence, "Phototherapy," Belfast Exposed, 2005. www.belfastexposed.org/themedpackages/index.php?id=2&sid=94&pid=22.

52. Jo Spence, "Photo Therapy and Breast Cancer—A Selection of Spence's Work," Breast Cancer Awareness, September 1996. http://hosted.aware.easynet.co.uk/jospence/jo1.htm.

53. Quoted in Hoy, *The Book of Photography*, p. 335.

54. Quoted in Adam Mazur and Paulina Skirgajllo-Krajewska, "If I Want to Take a Picture, I Take It No Matter What," Foto Apeta, 2003. http://fototapeta.art.pl/2003/ngie.php.

Chapter 5: Pixels and Pictures

55. Hoy, *The Book of Photography*, p. 401.

56. Quoted in Garner, *Disappearing Witness*, p. 249.

57. Pedro Meyer, "So Where Does Painting Start and Photography End?" ZoneZero, January 2006. http://zonezero.com/editorial/editorial.html.

58. John Goto, "Embarkation from Ham," John Goto's Gallery, 2006. www.johngoto.org.uk/floodscapes/floodscapes1.htm#.

59. Quoted in Melissa Denes, "Picture Perfect," *Guardian*, October 15, 2005. http://arts.guardian.co.uk/features/story/0,,1592506,00.html.

60. Jed Perl, "The Invisible Made Visible," *New Republic*, October 9, 2002. www.tnr.com/doc.mhtml?i=artnotes&s=perl100702.

61. J.D. Jarvis, "Digital Paint and Draw: Natural Media," Museum of Computer Art, November 2002. http://moca.virtual.museum/editorial/jdtour.htm#pt.9.

62. Jarvis, "Digital Paint and Draw."

63. Quoted in J.D. Jarvis, "An Art Lover's Guide to Digital Art," Museum of Computer Art, November 2002. http://moca.virtual.museum/editorial/jdessay.htm.

Important Dates

1826: French inventor Joseph Nicéphore Niépce takes the first photograph, a picture of the courtyard at his country estate in the village of St. Loup-de-Varennes.

1839: Louis-Jacques-Mandé Daguerre invents the daguerreotype photograph.

March 15, 1840: In New York City, Alexander Wolcott and John Johnson open the world's first portrait studio.

February 1851: Frederick Archer formulates the wet-plate collodion process, quickly recognized as superior, faster, and cheaper than the daguerreotype.

1871: English physician Richard Leach Maddox discovers the gelatin dry-plate process, which allows for smaller cameras and faster exposure times.

1888: George Eastman invents flexible, dry-roll film and sells it in the easy-to-operate Kodak camera.

1900: Kodak introduces the Brownie camera, a simple box camera that can be operated even by young children.

1902: Alfred Stieglitz forms the Photo-Secession movement with an elite group of photographers, including Gertrude Käsebier, Edward Steichen, Alvin Langdon Coburn, and Clarence H. White.

1925: Leica introduces the 35mm camera, which could shoot up to forty pictures on a single roll of film.

1927: The flashbulb is invented.

1932: The Group f/64 photography movement is founded in California by Ansel Adams. Members included Imogen Cunningham, Consuelo Kanaga, Sonya Noskowiak, and Edward Weston.

1936: *Life* magazine begins publication. Within a few years it becomes the best-selling photographic magazine in the world.

August 15, 1945: Alfred Eisenstaedt shoots "V-J Day," an iconic picture of a joyous sailor stealing an impromptu kiss from a nurse in Times Square while celebrating the end of World War II.

1958: Robert Frank publishes *The Americans*, a book filled with grainy, poorly exposed, and blurry photos that break many traditional rules of photography.

1967: The Museum of Modern Art in New York City holds the New Documents exhibition featuring work by Diane Arbus, Garry Winogrand, and Lee Friedlander.

February 1, 1968: AP photographer Eddie Adams takes the photograph "Murder of a Vietcong by Saigon Police Chief," a picture credited with helping turn public opinion against the Vietnam War.

1973: William Eggleston exhibits "Red Ceiling," produced with maximum color saturation, and becomes the "father of color photography."

1990: Robert Mapplethorpe's The Perfect Moment exhibition generates widespread controversy for displaying seven sexually explicit photos of gay men.

1991: Kodak sells the first digital camera, the DCS-100, attached to a huge side pack with a 200 MB hard drive capable of storing 156 images.

2000: The first cell phone cameras are sold.

2007: More than three-quarters of all cameras sold are digital and 70 percent of all professionally taken photographs are digital images.

Glossary

aperture: A ring of adjustable, overlapping, thin metal blades inside a camera lens. Photographers regulate the amount of light hitting the film by turning a ring on the barrel of the lens in order to change aperture settings.

calotype: A photographic process that produces a paper negative that can be used to make numerous prints on specially treated paper.

camera obscura: The forerunner of the modern camera, a box (which may be room-size) with a hole in one side. Light passes through the hole and creates an upside-down image on the back wall of the box.

charge-coupled device (CCD): An integrated circuit used in digital cameras capable of recording pixels, or picture elements, and converting them into information that can be read by a computer.

composition: The way in which elements of a visual image are arranged.

contrast: The difference between the lightest and darkest parts of a visual image.

daguerreotype: One of the earliest photographic processes, using a mirror-polished plate coated with photosensitive silver halide particles.

diorama: A theatrical representation of a scene created with artistic lighting, translucent material such as linen, paintings, and other effects.

gelatin emulsion: A substance used to apply photosensitive chemicals to glass plates or strips of celluloid film.

halftone printing: The process of transforming the gray tones or colors of a photograph into a series of small dots so they can be reproduced on a printing press. Halftone photographs are used in books, newspapers, magazines, and other printed material.

hyperrealism: A style of photography that uses realism to achieve a striking effect.

juxtaposition: The act of placing two or more things together in order to suggest a link between them or emphasize the contrast between them.

mise-en-scène: A term used to describe the positioning of actors, scenery, and props on a stage set to create a particular scene.

negative: Photographic film or plates that have been exposed to light, used to create prints. In a photographic negative, dark and light tones are reversed.

panorama: In its original form, a large circular painting that exhibits a wide view of an entire city.

photo-collage: A large artistic composition made from pieces of photographs, magazine clippings, objects such as machine parts, and other items.

photomontage: A photograph that consists of separate images that have been artfully combined to produce a single picture.

pigment: A substance that is used to give paint or ink its color.

pixel: A tiny dot of light that is the basic unit from which images on a computer monitor or television screen are made.

resolution: The level of detail reproduction, measured in pixels, offered by a computer chip, monitor, printer, scanner, or television.

saturation: The intensity of a color.

shutter: The mechanical part of a camera that opens and closes to expose the film or plate to light.

single-lens reflex (SLR): A camera that uses mirrors to provide the photographer with through-the-lens viewing.

staging: The process of positioning models in costumes with props and backdrops to create a photographic scene.

still life: A visual representation of inanimate objects such as fruit, flowers, or food in an artistic arrangement.

wet-plate collodion process: A photographic process using light-sensitive potassium iodide salts suspended in a thick, syrupy liquid called a collodion that is applied to a glass plate and exposed to light.

wirephoto: A term for the process of sending a halftone photograph through telephone or telegraph lines to distant media outlets.

For Further Reading

Books

Ansel Adams, *Ansel Adams California.* Boston: Little, Brown, 1997. This book features many rarely seen images of California taken by one of its most renowned photographers. The stunning photos are accompanied by a selection of writings about the state by classic and contemporary authors, including Robert Louis Stevenson, Mark Twain, John Muir, John Steinbeck, and Joan Didion.

Christopher C.L. Anderson, *Margaret Bourke-White: Adventurous Photographer.* New York: Franklin Watts, 2005. The story of one of the first photographers for *Life* magazine. Considered a pioneer in her field, Bourke-White captured images of many important events of the twentieth century, including World War II.

John Bankston, *Louis Daguerre and the Story of the Daguerreotype.* Hockessin, DE: Mitchell Lane, 2005. An exploration of the work done by Louis-Jacques-Mandé Daguerre, who experimented for years with the camera obscura and various chemicals and metals in order to perfect the world's first photographic method.

Alan Buckingham, *Digital Photo Magic.* New York: Dorling Kindersley, 2005. A guide to the digital camera, how it works, and how to obtain interesting special effects.

Ann Graham Gaines, *American Photographers: Capturing the Image.* Berkeley Heights, NJ: Enslow, 2002. Biographical information and photographs from renowned photographers such as Mathew B. Brady, Jacob A. Riis, Alfred Stieglitz, Lewis Wickes Hine, Man Ray, Dorothea Lange, Ansel Adams, Margaret Bourke-White, and Diane Arbus.

Neil Johnson, *National Geographic Photography Guide for Kids.* Washington, DC: National Geographic Society, 2001. An instructional guide explaining how a camera sees, how to use the frame, how to compose a picture and capture a moment, and how to move beyond snapshots to take pictures like a professional.

Elizabeth Partridge, *Restless Spirit: The Life and Work of Dorothea Lange.* New York: Viking, 1998. A biography of Dorothea Lange, whose photographs of migrant workers, Japanese American internees, and rural poverty inspired important social reforms. The book contains sixty photos and a text filled with Lange's own words.

Lynda Pflueger, *George Eastman: Bringing Photography to the People.* Berkeley

Heights, NJ: Enslow, 2002. Follows the life and career of the man who revolutionized photography by developing a camera simple enough for anyone to use.

Ingrid Schaffner, *The Essential Man Ray*. New York: Wonderland, 2003. A look at the life and times of the surrealist photographer and painter, one of the most famous American expatriate artists of the twentieth century. Contains 116 photos.

Web Sites

Diane Arbus: An Unofficial Website (www.dianearbus.net/index.htm). A site featuring photos, a biography, and favorable criticism of one of the most influential portrait photographers of the post–World War II era.

Don Archer, MOCA: Museum of Computer Art, University of the State of New York (http://moca.virtual.museum/index.asp). One of the most heavily trafficked, comprehensive, and respected computer art museums on the Web, MOCA promotes computer art in its various forms, including 3-D rendered art, fractals, enhanced photography, animation, mixed media, and computer-painted and -drawn art.

John Goto, New World Circus (www.johngoto.org.uk/NewWorldCircus/index.html). A series of digital photomontages created as a commentary on the Iraq war.

Library of Congress, "America from the Great Depression to World War II" (http://memory.loc.gov/ammem/fsahtml/fahome.html). A site with over 160,000 black-and-white photographs commissioned by the Farm Security Administration and the Office of War Information. This collection, a landmark in the history of documentary photography, shows rural and small-town American life and the adverse effects of the Great Depression and the dust bowl. The renowned photographers include Walker Evans, Dorothea Lange, and Roy Stryker.

New York Public Library Digital Gallery (http://digitalgallery.nypl.org/nypldigital/index.cfm). This Web site provides access to over 520,000 images digitized from primary sources and printed rarities in the collections of the New York Public Library, including manuscripts, historical maps, vintage posters, rare prints, and photographs of city life, workers, immigrants, children, and cultural events dating back to the 1850s.

Robert Altman, Le Photo Galerie (www.altmanphoto.com/PhotoGallery.html). The work of the former *Rolling Stone* photographer whose pictures of hippies, rock stars, and celebrities from the 1960s and 1970s are among the most expressive and celebrated of that era.

Vivid Light Photography (www.vividlight.com). A monthly online photography magazine with more than 1,200 articles on camera, darkroom, and Photoshop techniques; different photographic styles, including travel, portraiture, nature, and fashion; and more.

ZoneZero, "From Analog to Digital" (http://zonezero.com). A site founded by Pedro Meyer, a pioneer in contemporary photography, ZoneZero hosts the work of more than a thousand photographers from all over the world.

Index

Picture Credits

Cover: © Paul Mounce/CORBIS

© Alinari Archives/ CORBIS, 36
© Ansel Adams Publishing Rights
    Trust/CORBIS, 47
© Anthony Bolante/Reuters/CORBIS, 73
AP Images, 89
© Bettmann/CORBIS, 9, 27, 63, 85
© CORBIS, 52
Courtesy of the Henry Ford Museum and
    Greenfield Village, 12
© Historical Picture Archive/CORBIS,
    25
© James L. Amos/CORBIS, 83
© Leonard de Selva/CORBIS, 10
The Library of Congress, 50, 55
Margaret Bourke-White/Time Life
    Pictures/Getty Images, 53, 57
© Maurizio Gambarini/epa/CORBIS, 75
© Michael Freeman/CORBIS, 14
National Archives and Records
    Administration, 60

© NMPFT/SSPL/The Image Works, 28,
    67
Paul Strand/George Eastman House/
    Hulton Archive/Getty Images, 41
Peter Widing/AFP/Getty Images, 79
Photo by Hulton Archive/Getty Images, 18
Photo by James L. Amos/National
    Geographic/Getty Images, 23
Photo by Koichi Kamoshida, Getty
    Images, 84
Photo by MJ Kim/Getty Images, 76
Photo by Roger Viollet Collection/Getty
    Images, 16
Photo by Sean Sexton/Hulton
    Archive/Getty Images, 20
Photo by William Henry Fox
    Talbot/Hulton Archive/ Getty
    Images, 22
© RPS/Topham-HIP/The Image Works,
    39
© Science Museum/SSPL/The Image
    Works, 33, 34, 86

About the Author

Stuart A. Kallen is the author of more than two hundred non-fiction books for children and young adults. He has written on topics ranging from the theory of relativity to the history of rock and roll. In addition, Mr. Kallen has written award-winning children's videos and television scripts. In his spare time, Stuart A. Kallen is a singer/songwriter/guitarist in San Diego, California.